Kitchen Notes

Our test kitchen here in Sydney uses metric measurements. We have tested, retested and tested again to make these recipes fail proof. In all recipes we have given both metric and imperial measurements.

A 'cup' refers to a metric cup (250 ml/9 fl oz) and a 'tablespoon' is a metric tablespoon (20 ml/¾ fl oz). A teaspoon is 5 ml.

For many recipes the difference between the imperial and metric cup will be inconsequential; however, for cake, biscuit and pastry recipes, we highly recommend weighing ingredients using a digital scale as this will give the best possible results. To keep things simple, we have only given measurements in grams, ounces and cups where precision is essential.

1 lemon, juiced, yields approximately 50 ml (2½ tablespoons) of juice
1 stick of butter = 8 (US) tablespoons = 113.5 g = 4 oz
Eggs are 67–70 g (2⅓–2½ oz)
All herbs are fresh, unless otherwise indicated.
1 sachet dried yeast = 1 envelope dried yeast = 7 g = 2¼ teaspoons

MONDAY MORNING COOKING CLUB

The Feast Goes On

Lisa Goldberg, Merelyn Frank Chalmers, Natanya Eskin,
Lauren Fink, Paula Horwitz and Jacqui Israel

Photography Alan Benson
Styling David Morgan
Design Tania Gomes

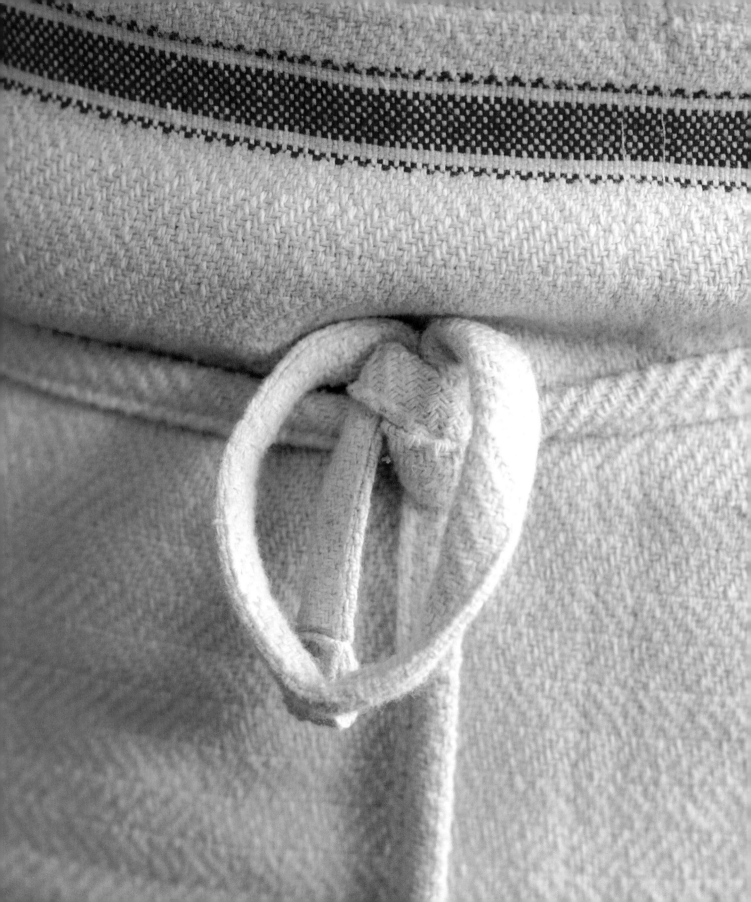

Contents

Our Story continues as the feast goes on...

We planted a seed of an idea in March 2006. Six women came together every Monday morning over endless cups of tea to find recipes with soul, recipes that might be lost, recipes that tell the story of a community: a community where it is always about the food. We knew we wanted to raise money for charity and we dreamed of writing a cookbook that could stand alongside any of the great cookbooks of the world. Using our combined skills of cooking, fressing and perseverance, we slowly grew that tiny seed into our dream.

Monday Morning Cooking Club: the food, the stories, the sisterhood was the culmination of five years of searching, collecting, testing, tasting, selecting, perfecting, shooting, writing and editing. And of course that one thing we excel at – debating. It is a unique snapshot of Sydney's Jewish community, an anthology of some of our best cooks who most generously shared their treasured recipes.

Its release in April 2011 was like the birth of a collective (between us all) eighteenth child. We were like first-time mothers, anxiously watching our baby's first steps into the world. We pinched ourselves time and time again when the cooks loved seeing their recipes in print, when people told us the food reminded them of their grandmothers and when the media made a fuss. We pinched ourselves again when we saw it in bookstore windows and on front shelf displays. And pinched ourselves again when it became our readers' go-to book and the recipes were being cooked over and over again.

We were inspired, excited and encouraged. We wanted to take our search for treasured recipes past the Sydney borders, across the whole country: to South Australia and to Perth in the west, to Queensland in the north and to Melbourne in the south. It was time for a second child: another book. The call went out and we were inundated with recipes from all over the country, hundreds and hundreds in fact; each and every one of them a delight to behold and a treasured insight.

The ordinary of many is the extraordinary of others. How privileged we felt to have a glimpse into what graces kitchen tables each night, a peek into special occasion dishes and favourites for Shabbat and Pesach. How honoured we felt to have access to life stories that are at times sad and tragic, luminous and special, familiar and comforting, strange and surprising; stories of survival and success, families and friends, loss and recovery; tales of grandmothers and daughters, of mothers and aunts, of fathers and friends. So many recipes handed down, a reminder forever of a loved one long gone.

Choosing recipes for this volume was a difficult job that weighed heavily on our shoulders. Culling was hard, and we were often emotionally attached to the cooks as well as the dishes. We wish we could have included every recipe but we had very strict criteria including genre, ease of making, size and space requirements. For every one we included in this book, there were five we were sad not to include. Sorry to all those generous, kind and amazing home cooks who submitted recipes that we were unable to use.

For those of you who have *the food, the stories, the sisterhood*, maybe it's time to put it aside for a while and play with this exciting new volume. You'll find that the books complement each other perfectly. For those of you meeting us for the first time, this book is a great place to start.

This volume has six chapters, which evolved after much lively debate, over many more cups of tea with introspection into how we, as a community, like to cook and eat. Coincidentally, or perhaps karmically, when we stood back to look at our chapter choices, it dawned on us that each chapter was indeed a true reflection of each one of us.

'Lunchtime' reflects Lauren, drawn to long Sunday lunches with a spread worthy of a magazine shoot. Jacqui is 'Everyday', all about efficiency and getting the job done – feeding her family and friends with much love and the minimum of fuss. Natanya adores 'Comfort'. She is happiest looking for and remembering the dishes that cause a flutter in the heart and satisfaction in the soul. Paula is always 'Feasting', preparing huge Shabbat dinner tables abundant with food and flowers, fit for a king. Lisa loves 'Fressing', she eats with joy and abandon, just going back for one more slice and enticing everyone else to join in. Merelyn holds strongly to 'Tradition', her time in the kitchen moving seamlessly from one Jewish festival to the next, committed to preserving the traditions of generations past for the future.

May these recipes fill your homes with heartwarming and luscious dishes. May you, and your friends and family, feel nurtured, nourished and loved just from the eating. May our stories inspire, engage and move you, and give you a unique insight into our extraordinary community.

The MMCC girls xx

The Sisterhood

Each one of the six of us shares in this book the story of someone close to our heart who still stands beside us in the kitchen, either literally or spiritually. For Lisa it is an aunt and for Merelyn a mother, both so sorely missed. For Natanya, Paula and Jacqui it is a mother, still a strong part of their lives and for Lauren, an inimitable mother-in-law. We are proud and honoured to share a snippet of their lives and our favourite recipes that will now live on forever.

Lisa Goldberg

I am the first to admit I am a fresser: dreaming, shopping, cooking, sharing, searching, ogling and photographing food and, of course, eating. I started professional life as a solicitor; since 2006 I have expressed this passion for food, cooking and preserving recipes in heading the Monday Morning Cooking Club project. This project has changed my life and taken my obsession with food to a whole new level. I equally love standing at my stove trying something new as much as making my old favourites that no longer need a recipe.

My food inspiration stems a little from my mum, Paula, a little more from my bubba, Shendel, and my mother-in-law, Talia, but mostly from my Aunty Myrna. My father's older sister, who passed away in 2004, was a horserace-loving, cigarette-smoking, platinum blonde with a heart bigger than any. Polish-born, she immigrated to Melbourne as a young child in the 1930s with my father and their family. She had a wonderful broad Australian Carlton accent with just a hint of Eastern Europe. After Myrna married, she and her husband, Sol, ran a tiny shop – part newsagent and part delicatessen – where truck drivers and locals lined up for her superb homemade European delicacies.

Sitting at her vinyl-clothed kitchen table with the 'wireless' on and the form guide open, she would force-feed me rugelach, tiny sultana strudels, butter chiffon. I regret that my serious interest in her recipes came too late. Many of them are now lost and will never be made again. I miss her greatly but it is through the few recipes I did write down that she now stands beside me in my kitchen, beaming. And when I make her simple cabbage rolls (page 120) and sweet tzimmes (page 267) for my husband, Danny, and my four children, Aunty Myrna joins us at the table.

Merelyn Frank Chalmers

Food is love and love is food. That's just the way it is for me. I grew up in a family that treasured food. My parents had experienced hunger, malnutrition and starvation during the war, and wanted that their children should never experience the same. My mother, Yolan, was always checking if I was hungry, telling me which foods were nutritious and delicious and pleading for me to put on a bit of weight.

Food was my link to my parents' home countries, a link to their spirituality, a link to their parents long gone. Stories came of my Polish grandmother, the best cook imaginable in my father's eyes. Never a particularly emotive man, he would swell with pride when he spoke of her gefilte fish and thick soups. My Hungarian mother arrived in Australia not having cooked much at all. She slowly but surely gathered Austro-Hungarian recipes that warmed her soul. One of my most treasured possessions is her old, weathered and yellowed notebook with recipes painstakingly written out by hand in Hungarian. Her avocado dip (page 207) and apple pie (page 224) can now live on forever.

Monday Morning Cooking Club inspired me to properly document my mother's recipes. I stood with her in the kitchen and watched and learned while my daughter Eliza captured it all in pictures. I am eternally grateful to the project for spurring me on.

I have a very different food philosophy to my mother's, yet we have a common thread. I believe that anything homemade must be good for you. Like her, I have an aversion to packaged food with long lists of ingredients and ply my family with my notion of health food. And like my mother, I believe most of the world's problems can be solved with a pot of well-brewed tea, a slice of cake and a dollop of cream.

Natanya Eskin

One of my strongest childhood memories is of my mum, Ruth, standing in the kitchen, wearing an apron and holding a wooden spoon. Now I am the one in an apron with my own children asking to lick the spoon.

Mum came to Australia at eighteen, accompanying her grandmother on a holiday. She met my father, they married, and three children later settled into Sydney's North Shore Jewish community. She created a traditional home, celebrating all the festivals and important occasions in our lives more with food than religion. She learned her best cooking secrets from both her Russian-Shanghai mother-in-law, Betty (Nanna), and her English mother, Sarah (Booba), and from her close friends.

I will always treasure the memory of standing with my mother, pen and paper in hand, watching Booba tap into her Polish heritage. She would make her amazing chopped liver, using an old-fashioned mincer, and chicken schmaltz.

Still today, Mum can always be depended upon for her countless traditional dishes that add so much richness and soul to our table. Matzo balls and chocolate date torte (page 187) at Pesach, gefilte fish (page 256), and Booba's chopped liver and honey cake at Rosh Hashanah.

The many years with my mother in the kitchen instilled in me, perhaps by osmosis, a love of baking. I am so passionate about cooking and feeding my family, just like my grandmothers before me. Thanks to this passion, I am an integral part of the Monday Morning Cooking Club and love being able to spend so many hours searching for recipes, working in the kitchen testing dishes and sharing the secrets of a community. The kitchen is my place of solace. Cooking for family and friends brings not only pleasure but beautiful childhood memories and bittersweet memories of loved ones no longer with us.

Lauren Fink

I love to feed my family and friends good, simple food. And plenty of it! My husband, Bruce, and our three children are definitely my greatest fans when it comes to my cooking and are all the inspiration and motivation I need. Growing up in South Africa, always surrounded by my mother's and grandmother's beautiful, plentiful food, the pattern was set. My mum, Melanie, always cooks from the heart, making us all feel nurtured and loved.

My mother-in-law, Yvonne Fink, with her larger-than-life personality, also cooks from the heart and is known for her most delicious *hamisher* food. Her chicken balls (page 79) and cholent (page 265) are now legendary in the family. Born in Melbourne, at eighteen she married Leon, a Polish immigrant, and, with the help of her own Polish bubba, Golda, she was introduced to wonderful Eastern European dishes. It was time she learned to cook; after all, she had Leon's family to impress. Bubba set about teaching Yvonne to be the best *Yiddishe* mamma, encouraging her to cook all the favourites from the home country. Being a good cook gave her great confidence, especially at such a young age.

Bruce and I used to visit often in our early years of marriage, staying in the guestroom next to the kitchen. I can still smell the wonderful aromas that emanated from there.

It's funny how one generation follows in the footsteps of the last. Yvonne tells us how the family used to get together every weekend for lunch, everyone would bring different dishes and they would sit and fress. My life is no different. We spend many weekends with friends and family, and it always seems to revolve around the food.

Paula Horwitz

My love for food, family and entertaining began decades ago, when, as a young barefooted kid, I would spend the holidays running around my aunt's sugarcane farm in the Natal midlands. I can still smell the roasting lamb with garlic and rosemary wafting out of the farmhouse kitchen windows. The wood-fired oven would produce delicious roasts with crisp potatoes and vegetables from the patch. Fruit salad was made from whatever we picked that day in the orchard. The family would gather around the dining table with cousins and siblings, enjoying my aunt's wonderful cooking. She was an amazing woman – running the farm by day and still finding the time to produce jams, pickled onions, relishes and conserves, which she would sell to keep the farm prosperous.

Our kitchen and home today resembles in many ways the style in which I was brought up. My mum, Sue, who has always been an accomplished cook, just like her sister, would cook lunch for my dad most days, who would come home from the office to enjoy it. She still makes traditional dishes that I prepare and recreate for my husband, Gary, and our three boys. They have a great appetite for Mum's recipes, particularly her cottage pie, oxtail, Durban curries, chocolate chip cookies, Dutch spice biscuits (page 240), melktart (page 141) and the world's best macaroni cheese.

Gary and I enjoy nothing more than entertaining our friends with great and plentiful food and a few glasses of wine. Gary is the real chef at our place but with me being part of the Monday Morning Cooking Club sisterhood, and together with my mother's influence, I have a newfound interest in cooking and he has a new rival in the kitchen.

Jacqui Israel

Entertaining has become my thing. It wasn't always the case but my immersion into the Monday Morning Cooking Club sisterhood has given me the confidence to cook … and now I cannot stop.

Breakfasts, brunches, lunches, afternoon teas and dinners – I love them all. I've mastered the art of planning ahead, being organised and working out what is best for different types of entertaining.

I have lived in Sydney all my life, growing up with English-born parents. As a child, I was given the task of preparing the family meal once a week, which made me step outside my comfort zone and search for and experiment with new recipes. I was inspired by my grandmothers' kitchens, which were always overflowing with different and tantalising foods. I looked forward to Shabbat dinners and as we drove the 45 minutes to get over the Harbour Bridge through bumper-to-bumper Friday night traffic, it gave me time to dream of what would be served. My Nana Rene would ply us all with huge amounts of food until we were stuffed to the brim. The drive home always went quickly because I would fall asleep on the back seat, satisfied and full.

My mum, Sylvie, has mastered some favourites of my grandmother's recipes. One of the most special is her beetroot jam (page 250) – a viscous, sticky and sweet jam for Pesach. And of course we love the coconut macaroons (page 285), which originally were pyramid shaped for Pesach, but now I make them as moreish little coconut morsels.

I do hope to pass on my love of cooking to my daughter, Lexi, and son, James, as food is a wonderful way to bring family and friends together.

Lunchtime

Friends for lunch. Relaxed entertaining with an easy and modern style that reflects my generation. The joy I get from sharing laughter and friendship in my home. The table laden with huge platters of fresh produce, colourful salads to share. Just-poached salmon flaked over crisp greens drizzled with a beautiful dressing, a loaf of local sourdough bread and a bottle or two of rosé. What could be a better way to spend a Sunday?

Lauren xxx

Recipes

{Ruby's eggplant and Israeli couscous salad}

This salmon is representative of the best way to eat, the simplest preparation with the best ingredients. The versatility of this dish is the many ways to serve it: as a breakfast with eggs, as a lunch or dinner with beautiful salads, or simply on some local sourdough with a handful of green leaves and a splash of first season pressed extra virgin olive oil.

Salmon pastrami

1 TABLESPOON BLACK
    PEPPERCORNS
1 TABLESPOON CORIANDER SEEDS
75 G (¼ CUP) SALT
110 G (½ CUP) SUGAR
1 SIDE OF ATLANTIC SALMON,
    ABOUT 1 KG (2 LB 4 OZ), SKINNED
    AND PIN-BONED
WOOD-FIRED OR SOURDOUGH
    BREAD, TOASTED, FOR SERVING
LEMON WEDGES, FOR
    GARNISHING
EXTRA VIRGIN OLIVE OIL, FOR
    SERVING

SPICE CRUST
1½ TABLESPOONS BLACK
    PEPPERCORNS
1½ TABLESPOONS YELLOW
    MUSTARD SEEDS
1¼ TABLESPOONS CORIANDER SEEDS

Start this recipe 2 days before serving.

Coarsely crush the peppercorns and coriander seeds with a mortar and pestle or in a food processor. Place with the salt and sugar in a small bowl and mix until well combined. Rub this mixture all over the salmon and transfer to a ceramic or other non-reactive dish. Cover with plastic wrap and place in the fridge for 24 hours. There will be a lot of liquid in the dish which you do not need to remove. Turn the salmon over and return to the fridge for another 24 hours.

Remove the salmon from the fridge and drain away any liquid. Use a dry pastry brush and paper towel to brush off any excess curing mixture.

To make the spice crust, use a mortar and pestle or spice grinder to crush the peppercorns, mustard seeds and coriander seeds. Place in a small bowl and mix until well combined. Press the spice mixture onto both sides of the salmon fillet to form a thick crust. Cover tightly with plastic wrap and refrigerate until ready to slice.

To serve, finely slice the salmon from head to tail on a 45-degree angle. Arrange on a platter with the toasted bread and lemon wedges and drizzle with the olive oil.

Serves 20 as an hors d'oeuvres

Food has always played an essential role in my life. Born in Johannesburg, South Africa, I have wonderful memories of travelling to Cape Town each December holiday and walking into my maternal grandmother's pantry. There I found, to my delight, shelves from floor to ceiling stacked with biscuit tins, every kind imaginable, each filled with homemade treats made with so much love for her precious grandchildren. And of my paternal grandmother's home; our family sitting around the dining table on the yomtovim eating the very same family favourites that we all still adore today. Mum threw extraordinary dinner parties with fabulous food, everything presented exquisitely.

In 2006 I made Sydney my home. When I started my catering business soon after I moved here, my greatest joy was to serve food that tasted as delicious as it looked beautiful.

Today I love to share my table with family and friends, which fills my soul with joy.

BRENDA GORDON

I am so lucky to come from a line of extraordinary cooks; when my first two sons were born, there were five generations and we all loved gathering around the dining table. My mother, Sybil, had the best tastebuds of all of us. Often when I was trying a new recipe, I would phone her and say, 'It just doesn't taste quite right.' She would come over straight away and add a little something to make it just perfect.

I immigrated to Australia in 2002 to live closer to my children, and I must say, I have loved Sydney since the day I arrived. For the last ten years, I have owned Bianca's Deli in Rose Bay with my daughter Shelley and son-in-law Barry. We specialise in traditional Jewish cooking, South African food products and home-cooked meals, but our most popular product is probably biltong. I am so happy when customers come into the deli and tell me how much they love my food. But I am happiest when my family come for dinner and say, 'Beanie, the food was delicious.'

I've always loved entertaining and experimenting to create special new recipes for family and friends. This recipe is the result of a very successful experiment and has become a regular favourite at my table.

Mushroom and zucchini roll

PASTRY
375 G (13 OZ/2½ CUPS) PLAIN (ALL-
   PURPOSE) FLOUR
¼ TEASPOON SALT
250 G (9 OZ) COLD BUTTER,
   CHOPPED
250 ML (1 CUP) PURE CREAM
   (35% FAT)

FILLING
½ ONION, FINELY CHOPPED
60 G (2¼ OZ) BUTTER
500 G (1 LB 2 OZ) BUTTON
   MUSHROOMS, SLICED
350 G (12 OZ) ZUCCHINIS
   (COURGETTES), GRATED
1 TABLESPOON PLAIN (ALL-PURPOSE)
   FLOUR
125 ML (½ CUP) MILK
SEA SALT AND FRESHLY GROUND
   BLACK PEPPER

1 EGG, BEATEN, TO GLAZE
2 TABLESPOONS SESAME SEEDS

To make the pastry, place the flour and salt in a food processor. Add the butter and process until you have coarse crumbs. Pour in the cream and process for a couple of minutes until a ball of dough forms. Wrap in plastic wrap and refrigerate for 30 minutes before rolling out.

Preheat the oven to 200°C (400°F/Gas 6). Line a baking tray.

To make the filling, heat a frying pan over medium heat and fry the onion in the butter until soft and golden. Add the mushrooms and cook until soft and golden brown and most of the liquid has evaporated. Add the zucchini and cook for a minute or two. Stir in the flour and cook for 30 seconds. Stir in the milk and cook for a few minutes until the mixture thickens. Season generously to taste with salt and pepper. Allow to cool.

Cut the pastry in half and, on a floured bench, roll one piece into a rectangle. Spoon half the filling down the centre. Wrap the pastry over and first pinch together the ends with your fingers and then seal along the length of the roll. Repeat with the remaining dough and filling. Place the rolls, seam side down, on the prepared tray. To avoid splitting, cut three slits diagonally along the tops.

Brush each roll with the egg and sprinkle with the sesame seeds. Bake for 30–40 minutes until golden on top and cooked through underneath.

Serve warm or at room temperature.

Makes 2 rolls
Each roll serves 6–8

The sweet and sour of Italian cooking transforms capsicums into a delicious side dish. This is great as part of an antipasto platter, or as an accompaniment to grilled meat, chicken or fish.

Peperonata agrodolce

6 RED OR YELLOW CAPSICUMS (PEPPERS), OR A COMBINATION

2 SMALL RED ONIONS

80 ML (⅓ CUP) EXTRA VIRGIN OLIVE OIL

SEA SALT AND FRESHLY GROUND BLACK PEPPER

2 TABLESPOONS BABY CAPERS, RINSED AND DRAINED

2 TABLESPOONS RAISINS

125 ML (½ CUP) RED WINE VINEGAR

1 TABLESPOON SUGAR, OR TO TASTE

6–8 BASIL OR MINT LEAVES

Cut the capsicums in half lengthways, remove the seeds and chop into 2 cm (¾ inch) squares.

Slice the onions and put them in a large frying pan with the olive oil, capsicum, salt and pepper. Add the capers and raisins, cover and cook over low heat for about 15 minutes, stirring regularly.

Add the vinegar and sugar to the pan, stir and continue to simmer, uncovered, until the liquid has evaporated, about 30 minutes. Remove from the stove and add the basil or mint leaves.

Serve at room temperature.

Serves 4–6 as a side dish

My passion for food is intertwined with significant aspects of my life – in particular my family and travels, especially to Italy and Israel. I share all these passions with my loving wife, Rebecca.

My parents arrived in Sydney in 1949 after surviving the war; I was born here and have lived in Australia all my life. Food for me is about family and sharing with the important people in my life. Now that I'm a grandfather, my greatest pleasure is being able to prepare and cook handmade pasta with my grandchildren; a simple task, yet such a joy. I love to spend a chilly winter's day in the Blue Mountains cooking my best dishes: plenty of hearty soups, golden roast turkeys and creative, aromatic dishes. For me, that's what food is about – delicious, flavoursome tastes and creating warm and special memories.

These recipes come from time spent in Sicily, an island with exciting cultural diversity that is reflected in its food. We did a cooking course in the home of a delightful Italian lady who shared these recipes with us, which I have adapted over the years to suit my own tastes.

A dish that shines because of its simplicity; zucchini, lemon and salt is a wonderful combination. The thinner you can slice the zucchini, the more spectacular this salad becomes. Lovely as a side dish to any main meal, or as part of a salad selection at lunch.

Zucchine marinate

500 G (1 LB 2 OZ) ZUCCHINIS
   (COURGETTES)
SALT
JUICE OF 3 LEMONS
80 ML (⅓ CUP) EXTRA VIRGIN OLIVE
   OIL
1 CLOVE GARLIC, BRUISED
2 HANDFULS FLAT-LEAF (ITALIAN)
   PARSLEY, FINELY CHOPPED
1 LONG RED CHILLI, DESEEDED
   AND FINELY CHOPPED
FRESHLY GROUND BLACK PEPPER
100 G (3½ OZ) CACIOCAVALLO OR
   PARMESAN CHEESE, FINELY
   SHAVED

Finely slice the zucchini with either a vegetable peeler or mandoline. Sprinkle generously with the salt and set aside for 20 minutes.

Rinse the zucchini well under cold running water. Strain and pat dry on paper towel and put into a bowl. Add two-thirds of the lemon juice and leave to marinate for half an hour, stirring occasionally.

Meanwhile, make the dressing by mixing together the olive oil, garlic, parsley, chilli, pepper and the remaining lemon juice.

Strain the zucchini well and arrange on a serving dish. Drizzle the dressing over, removing the garlic clove, then sprinkle with the cheese. Serve at room temperature.

Serves 4–6 as a side dish

This onion tart recipe evolved from the apfel wehr, *my Swiss aunt's recipe for a traditional Swiss apple tart. Chilling the tart shell in the fridge for 2 hours before blind-baking will help prevent the pastry from shrinking.*

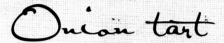

Onion tart

PASTRY
350 G (12 OZ/2⅓ CUPS) PLAIN
    (ALL-PURPOSE) FLOUR
180 G (6½ OZ) COLD UNSALTED
    BUTTER, CHOPPED
2 TABLESPOONS COLD WATER

FILLING
1 KG (2 LB 4 OZ/ABOUT 6) BROWN
    ONIONS, ROUGHLY CHOPPED OR
    SLICED
60 ML (¼ CUP) OLIVE OIL
4 EGG YOLKS
250 ML (1 CUP) PURE CREAM
    (35% FAT)
PINCH OF FRESHLY GRATED
    NUTMEG
SEA SALT AND FRESHLY GROUND
    BLACK PEPPER

You will need a 26–28 cm (10¼–11 inch) tart (flan) tin with a removable base.

To make the pastry, process the flour, butter and water together in a food processor for a few minutes until a rough dough forms. Remove, wrap in plastic wrap and refrigerate for 30 minutes.

Preheat the oven to 180°C (350°F/Gas 4).

Roll the dough out on a floured bench and gently press into the tin. Trim the pastry to fit and reserve the left-over pastry to patch any cracks.

To blind-bake the tart, line the pastry shell with foil and fill with baking weights or uncooked rice or beans. Bake until cooked, about 20 minutes. Remove the foil and weights and bake for an additional 15–20 minutes until lightly golden. If there are any cracks, patch with the left-over pastry.

While the tart shell is baking, prepare the filling.

In a large frying pan over low to medium heat, sauté the onion in the oil until very soft and light brown. This may take up to an hour. Set aside to cool slightly. Beat the egg yolks with the cream. Add the nutmeg and season well with salt and pepper. Stir the onion through the cream mixture.

Carefully fill the pastry shell with the filling, place in the oven and bake for 40–45 minutes, or until the filling is set.

Serve warm or at room temperature.

Serves 8

I was born in Melbourne in 1925 to a Russian father and Swiss mother. My mother was one of nineteen children herself, seven of whom immigrated to Australia with my grandmother. My mother was a very good cook. She prepared all the Jewish traditional foods for the festivals, but on a day-to-day basis she enjoyed more modern recipes – casseroles, pastas, crème caramel and so on.

In the 1960s I started a cooking school, The Complete Hostess, with my cousin Sonya Sicree. The school was held in Melbourne's well-known Chapel Street; many of our contemporaries attended those classes and still continue to use our recipes today.

I also worked in human resources and recruitment, eventually selling my company to an American multinational in the late 1980s. Feeling at a loss, I started a small business making chutneys and jams, reincarnating the name 'The Complete Hostess'. Eventually I retired from the kitchen and now enjoy my memories of time spent there.

YARON FINKELSTEIN

This salad originated from a time-honoured tradition: my wife, Ruby, made me do it! We both love Israeli couscous and one year, as her annual birthday lunch approached, she suggested I use it together with the bountiful thatch of mint and parsley we had bought to create a salad that could be served in large quantities, banquet style. The eggplant, slow roasted and then tinged with lemon, is the perfect nod to its Israeli origins.

Ruby's eggplant and Israeli couscous salad

1 MEDIUM EGGPLANT (AUBERGINE), **SKIN ON**

3 TEASPOONS GROUND CORIANDER

SEA SALT AND FRESHLY GROUND BLACK PEPPER

80 ML (⅓ CUP) **OLIVE OIL, PLUS EXTRA, IF NEEDED**

1 LARGE ONION, CHOPPED

1 CLOVE GARLIC, CRUSHED

250 G (9 oz) **ISRAELI** (PEARL) **COUSCOUS**

310 ML (1¼ CUPS) **VEGETABLE OR CHICKEN STOCK**

1 BUNCH CORIANDER (CILANTRO), **CHOPPED**

½ BUNCH FLAT-LEAF (ITALIAN) **PARSLEY, CHOPPED**

½ BUNCH MINT, CHOPPED

JUICE OF ½ LEMON, OR TO TASTE

Preheat the oven to 150°C (300°F/Gas 2). Line a baking tray.

Chop the eggplant into small cubes and place in a large mixing bowl with 1 teaspoon of the ground coriander and a little salt. Pour 2 tablespoons of the oil onto the eggplant, mix, then sprinkle on another teaspoon of coriander and another tablespoon of oil. Mix until the cubes are roughly coated with oil and spice and then place on the tray and into the oven. Roast for 25 minutes, then turn the eggplant cubes over and return to the oven again for another 25 minutes, or until brown, taking care to avoid burning. Set aside.

While the eggplant is roasting, gently sauté the onion in a saucepan with the remaining oil until soft and golden, then add the remaining ground coriander, the black pepper and garlic. Stir for 1 minute, or until fragrant. Add the couscous and stir until the grains are coated with the spice mix and lightly toasted. Add enough stock to cover the couscous and bring to the boil. Reduce the heat to very low and cover with a lid.

After 10 minutes, check the couscous, using a fork to fluff the grains. Loosen any grains stuck to the bottom of the pan. Cover again and cook for another 5 minutes. Fluff again and set aside, covered.

In a large bowl, mix together the couscous, herbs and eggplant. Stir in the lemon juice and a little extra olive oil if needed and season to taste. Serve warm or at room temperature.

Serves 6–8

Photo on page 22

YARON FINKELSTEIN

My earliest food memories are my most simple; sitting in the kitchen watching my mother make dinner and being asked to help, not hinder! I remember her frying chopped onion and garlic for her meatballs, which were gently shaped before adding to the pan. It was only years later that I decided she was adding the garlic too early, causing it to burn. What's a precocious teenage son for, if not to find a better way for his parents to do something they've been doing for years?

Ours is a classic story, so often shared by other Australian Jews from Europe. My Czech grandmother met my Polish grandfather waiting for resettlement in Italy following the devastation of the Second World War. Arriving in Palestine in 1947, they wed and looked forward to a fresh start. Born and raised in Israel, my parents waited until my father had finished his military service to make the long journey to Australia, where I was born.

Over time I have developed a near obsessive fascination with cooking, food history and the many varied cuisines I now modestly attempt to understand. My cookbook collection is bordering on unmanageable, though they help to provide my friends and family with fantastic meals and even better memories.

ROBYN KAUFMAN

Almost everything of significance in our family happens around food. In a big family with four kids, mealtimes, and the food itself, sets the beat, the rhythm, and the connection.

When I was younger and growing up in South Africa, I was more ambivalent about food and fought hard against the stereotype of being a woman in the kitchen. Despite this, memories of my childhood are completely connected to the pleasures of food prepared by my grandmother and mother, both amazing cooks. My father's mother, Ouma, would stay with us for the Jewish festivals and make soup and kneidlach and special pancakes with sugar and cinnamon, all while telling us the most fantastical stories.

Today, living in Sydney, there is nothing I enjoy more than everyone jammed into the kitchen, music playing, a bottle of wine open and all of us cooking together. Then, around the table, while we are enjoying our food, we are at our most intense – laughing, talking, discussing and debating, and not always in agreement of course!

Soups are a family favourite in winter. Roasting the vegetables produces a richer taste than the usual boiling. What I love about this soup is that by combining two sometimes plain ingredients, the result is such an interesting combination of flavours.

Roasted carrot and fennel soup

1 FENNEL BULB, TRIMMED,
   FRONDS RESERVED
4–5 CARROTS, PEELED AND
   SLICED
60 ML (¼ CUP) OLIVE OIL
SEA SALT AND FRESHLY GROUND
   BLACK PEPPER
1 TEASPOON FENNEL SEEDS
1 ONION, FINELY CHOPPED
1 TABLESPOON TOMATO PASTE
   (CONCENTRATED PURÉE)
1.25 LITRES (5 CUPS) VEGETABLE
   STOCK

Preheat the oven to 200°C (400°F/Gas 6).

Cut the fennel in half lengthways and then cut each half into wedges. Toss the carrot slices and fennel with 2 tablespoons of the olive oil and season well with salt and pepper. Spread evenly on a baking tray and bake for 30–45 minutes, or until brown and tender.

Meanwhile, toast the fennel seeds in a small frying pan over medium heat for 2–3 minutes, or until they turn lightly brown, then crush in a mortar and pestle.

Heat the remaining olive oil in a large saucepan over medium heat. Add the onion and crushed fennel seeds and cook for 10 minutes, or until the onion is soft and translucent. Reduce the heat to low and add the tomato paste, roasted vegetables and stock. Simmer for 10 minutes. Season with salt and pepper and allow to cool slightly. Purée with a stick blender or in a blender.

Reheat and serve garnished with the reserved chopped fennel fronds.

Serves 4–6

This salad is an all-time favourite of mine. It is relatively healthy, the combination of textures is amazing and it can be eaten as a vegetarian main or side dish.

Moroccan roast cauliflower salad

1 CAULIFLOWER, LEAVES
  REMOVED
1 TEASPOON CUMIN SEEDS
1 TABLESPOON OLIVE OIL, PLUS
  EXTRA, FOR DRIZZLING
1 TEASPOON GROUND CUMIN
½ TEASPOON DRIED CHILLI
  FLAKES
½ TEASPOON GROUND
  CORIANDER
SEA SALT AND FRESHLY GROUND
  BLACK PEPPER
1 BUNCH CORIANDER (CILANTRO),
  CHOPPED
75 G (½ CUP) MACADAMIA NUTS,
  ROUGHLY CHOPPED
200 G (7 OZ) FETA CHEESE,
  CRUMBLED

Preheat the oven to 180°C (350°F/Gas 4).

Cut the cauliflower in half and remove the stems, setting them aside. Divide half of the cauliflower into small florets. Chop the other half, together with all the stems, place in a food processor and process until it resembles uncooked couscous. Place them both in a large mixing bowl.

Toast the cumin seeds in a dry frying pan for 2 minutes, or until fragrant. Combine with the cauliflower, olive oil, spices, salt and pepper. Arrange in a single layer on a large baking tray and drizzle with a little extra olive oil. Bake for 45 minutes to 1 hour, or until golden brown and tender. Toss with the coriander, macadamias and feta.

Serve warm or at room temperature.

Serves 6

I was a vegetarian for over 30 years and so I always found myself looking for new ideas with interesting grains. This recipe combines a number of my favourite ingredients – peas, asparagus and red onion – and is really the epitome of the taste of summer.

Summer freekeh salad

3 RED ONIONS, FINELY SLICED INTO RINGS

30 G (1½ TABLESPOONS) CASTER (SUPERFINE) SUGAR

SEA SALT AND FRESHLY GROUND BLACK PEPPER

125 ML (½ CUP) BALSAMIC VINEGAR, PLUS EXTRA FOR DRIZZLING

3 TABLESPOONS EXTRA VIRGIN OLIVE OIL, PLUS EXTRA FOR DRIZZLING

400 G (14 OZ) PACKET FREEKEH

2 BUNCHES ASPARAGUS, TRIMMED

160 G (1 CUP) PEAS

½ BUNCH CORIANDER (CILANTRO), ROUGHLY CHOPPED

200 G (7 OZ) FETA CHEESE, CRUMBLED

Preheat the oven to 180°C (350°F/Gas 4).

Place the onion on a baking tray and sprinkle with the sugar, salt and pepper. Pour over the balsamic vinegar and drizzle with the olive oil. Roast for about 30 minutes, then toss and continue roasting until caramelised and golden, about 1 hour.

While the onion is cooking, rinse the freekeh well. Place in a saucepan and cover generously with water. Bring to the boil, reduce the heat to low, then simmer for 20–30 minutes, or until the freekeh is tender but still firm. Rinse and drain thoroughly. Place in a salad bowl.

Blanch the asparagus in boiling salted water for about 2 minutes, and then refresh immediately in cold water. Drain and cut into 2 cm (¾ inch) pieces.

Cook the peas in boiling salted water for 1 minute, then refresh.

Toss the caramelised onion with all its cooking juices through the freekeh. Add the asparagus and peas, then the coriander and feta. Season to taste with salt and pepper and, if necessary, dress with extra olive oil and balsamic vinegar. Serve at room temperature.

Serves 12

When making salads I have learned to adjust ingredients according to visual balance and personal likings. If a salad calls for feta cheese but someone loves goat's cheese, then I use that instead. I like to use a large, lightweight mixing bowl to toss the salad and then transfer it to the serving dish, adjusting for colour and appearance if needed.

Shaved fennel and mint salad

1 FENNEL BULB, ABOUT 450 G
(1 LB), FRONDS RESERVED
6–8 (160 G) SMALL RADISHES
6–8 (180 G) BRUSSELS SPROUTS
1½ CUPS (240 G) PEAS, BLANCHED
1 LONG RED CHILLI, DESEEDED
AND FINELY SLICED
1 LARGE HANDFUL MINT LEAVES,
TORN
100 G (1 HEAPED CUP) WALNUTS
150 G (5½ OZ) GOAT'S CHEESE,
CRUMBLED

DRESSING
100 ML (5 TBSP) LEMON JUICE
2 TABLESPOONS SHERRY VINEGAR
100 ML (SCANT ½ CUP) OLIVE OIL
¾ TEASPOON SEA SALT
FRESHLY GROUND BLACK PEPPER

Use a mandoline or sharp knife to very finely slice the fennel, radishes and brussels sprouts. Place in a bowl and add the peas, fennel fronds, chilli and mint. Toss together gently.

To make the dressing, in a small bowl, whisk together the lemon juice, sherry vinegar, olive oil, salt and pepper.

Toss the salad with the dressing, then garnish with the walnuts and goat's cheese.

Serves 8

I fell in love with food because of my late dad. He never ceased to amaze us with his wild culinary concoctions. I still remember waking up on a Sunday morning to the smells of his cooking wafting through the house. Dad cooked because he loved seeing others enjoying his food. I am the same, always encouraging people to try new things and simply being happy in the kitchen, cooking for my family of boys.

On weekends away with my lifelong girlfriends, it has become a tradition that I plan our menus – I put my 'sous chefs' to work with strict orders (they are usually pretty obedient!) and over a glass of wine we cook, laugh and cry together, and then sit down to enjoy the fruits of our labour. The next day we do it all again. I remember reading somewhere that your mood is captured in your cooking so I do believe my family and friends can taste the love I put into my food.

GEORGIA SAMUEL

Being an eighth-generation Australian, we grew up eating traditional Australian food. My husband, Adam, an incredible cook of Israeli heritage, introduced me to a whole realm of spices and Middle Eastern cooking. He was really the inspiration for my newfound interest in cooking.

I used to practise law at a large corporate law firm. Throughout my career, I joked with Adam that one day I would leave to open a salad bar. I saw a real gap in the market for delicious, healthy and filling food. I found myself devising salad recipes at 3 am instead of sleeping in preparation for the long day ahead of legal drafting! I woke up one morning and said to Adam, 'I'm going to do it!' He suggested we take a leave of absence to ensure I had made the right decision. We spent the next five months travelling around the UK, America and South America – mostly gathering ideas for the concept. Four days before I was due back, I resigned. In May 2010, I opened the first famish'd salad bar in the heart of Melbourne's CBD, and the second in 2013. Together with the birth of our daughter, it's certainly a change from the law.

{Middle Eastern crunch salad}

This salad started as a simple crunchy vegetable salad with our famous dressing at famish'd. Adam and I made it at home one day and added marinated chicken. We had some of Adam's Israeli father's homemade hummus in the fridge, so added that too. Little did we know, we were throwing together an incredible new salad.

Middle Eastern crunch salad

PARSLEY HUMMUS

250 G (1 HEAPED CUP) DRIED CHICKPEAS

240 G (1 CUP) HULLED TAHINI

2 CLOVES GARLIC, ROUGHLY CHOPPED

JUICE OF ½ LEMON, OR TO TASTE

60 ML (¼ CUP) EXTRA VIRGIN OLIVE OIL, PLUS EXTRA, FOR DRIZZLING

125 ML (½ CUP) WATER

1 VERY LARGE HANDFUL FLAT-LEAF (ITALIAN) PARSLEY

2 TEASPOONS SEA SALT

FRESHLY GROUND BLACK PEPPER

SWEET OR HUNGARIAN PAPRIKA

CHICKEN

80 ML (⅓ CUP) OLIVE OIL

1 TABLESPOON GROUND CUMIN

1 TABLESPOON GROUND CORIANDER

1 TABLESPOON GROUND CINNAMON

2 CLOVES GARLIC, CRUSHED

12 SKINLESS, BONELESS CHICKEN THIGH FILLETS

Start this recipe the day before if using dried chickpeas.

Soak the chickpeas in water overnight. Drain and rinse, then place in a saucepan and cover generously with water. Bring to the boil, then simmer for an hour, or until soft to bite. Rinse with cold water to stop cooking.

For the hummus, place the tahini, garlic, lemon juice, olive oil and water in a food processor and process until smooth. Add the chickpeas, parsley, salt and pepper and process for a few minutes until very smooth. If necessary, add more oil, water or lemon juice to suit your preferred consistency and taste. Taste for seasoning. Pour into a bowl and lightly stir the paprika through. Drizzle with olive oil to serve.

For the chicken, mix together the olive oil, cumin, coriander, cinnamon and garlic and rub into the chicken. Place in the fridge to marinate while you make the salad, or overnight if desired.

For the salad, cook the two types of rice in separate saucepans according to the packet instructions. Drain well and cool. Finely dice the capsicums, celery and spring onions into small pieces and place in a large mixing bowl. Toast the pine nuts in a frying pan over medium heat, tossing constantly, until lightly browned. Remove from the pan immediately and set aside to cool. Add the pine nuts, coriander and pomegranate seeds to the diced vegetables. Combine well with the rice and toss through the sunflower seeds.

SALAD

200 G (1 CUP) **BROWN RICE**

160 G (1 CUP) **WILD RICE**

1 EACH RED, GREEN AND YELLOW CAPSICUM (PEPPER)

8 SMALL CELERY STALKS

3 SPRING ONIONS (SCALLIONS)

150 G (1 CUP) **PINE NUTS**

1 HANDFUL CORIANDER (CILANTRO) **LEAVES, ROUGHLY CHOPPED**

SEEDS FROM 1 POMEGRANATE

130 G (1 CUP) **SUNFLOWER SEEDS**

DRESSING

60 ML (¼ CUP) **VEGETABLE OIL**

60 ML (¼ CUP) **SOY SAUCE**

JUICE OF 1 LEMON

1 TABLESPOON HONEY

1 CLOVE GARLIC, CRUSHED

FRESHLY GROUND BLACK PEPPER

For the dressing, combine all the ingredients and mix well.

Pour the dressing over the salad and toss. Tip onto a serving platter.

Barbecue or pan-fry the chicken until cooked through. Arrange on top of the salad and dollop some of the hummus on top. Serve the rest in a bowl alongside.

Leftovers will keep well stored in an airtight container in the fridge for several days.

Serves 8–10

NOTE: If time is limited, you can substitute 2 x 400g (14 oz) tins of chickpeas, rinsed well and drained, for the dried chickpeas.

Photo on page 45

Making the most of winter vegetables, this slaw is a staple in our repertoire – the balance between bitter leaves, sweet raisins and fresh herbs makes it a great accompaniment to roast chicken, barbecued meats or a slow-cooked stew.

Red cabbage and raisin slaw

¼ RED CABBAGE
1 FENNEL BULB
1 HEAD RADICCHIO OR TREVISO
1 BUNCH DILL, FRONDS ONLY
1 BUNCH FLAT-LEAF (ITALIAN)
  PARSLEY, LEAVES ONLY
80 G (½ CUP) RAISINS
80 G (½ CUP) PINE NUTS, TOASTED

DRESSING
2 TABLESPOONS LEMON JUICE
2 TABLESPOONS WHITE WINE
  VINEGAR
170 ML (⅔ CUP) EXTRA VIRGIN
  OLIVE OIL
1 TEASPOON SEA SALT

Finely shave the cabbage and fennel on a mandoline or with a sharp knife. Cut the radicchio or treviso in half, then finely slice to match the cabbage. Tear the dill fronds. Place all in a large bowl. Add the parsley, raisins and pine nuts.

To make the dressing, whisk the lemon juice, white wine vinegar, olive oil and salt in a small bowl or shake in a jar.

Dress the salad just before serving.

Serves 10–12

We were best friends in high school; we are now married and have recently started our own family. We both grew up in traditional Jewish homes steeped in food from our grandparents' memories. Recipes weren't written down but cooked from pre-war stories of Poland, Germany and Czechoslovakia. Our grandparents immigrated to Australia with nothing – for them, teaching us their traditions and family secrets was a way of remembering and sharing their heritage. Growing up in these kitchens, we've always had an appreciation for cooking with instinct and respect for the origin of a dish.

Cooking is a passion we share and relish; in 2011 we spent a year in London training at Leith's Cooking School. Although we now do private catering, I work as a genetic counsellor and Adam in marketing and ecommerce. We approach cooking with a focus on play and experimentation – we aim to utilise a scientific approach to our food while maintaining the essence of our ingredients. It is not unusual to walk into our kitchen and find anything from freshly churned butter and no-knead bread to 72-hour sous vide brisket.

I first tasted this wonderfully fresh salad years ago in a Lebanese restaurant and then recreated my own version. It's a winner for me, as anything with pomegranates or pomegranate molasses makes my mouth water. And it's a lovely change from all the cakes that I have come to know so intimately over the decades.

Fattoush

2 SLICES MOUNTAIN OR PITA
  BREAD
2 TEASPOONS OLIVE OIL
¼ ICEBERG (CRISPHEAD) LETTUCE,
  SHREDDED
500 G (1LB 2 OZ) CHERRY OR GRAPE
  TOMATOES, HALVED
3 RADISHES, VERY FINELY SLICED
5 FRENCH SHALLOTS, FINELY
  SLICED
2 LEBANESE (SHORT) CUCUMBERS,
  HALVED LENGTHWAYS AND
  FINELY SLICED
1 LARGE HANDFUL FLAT-LEAF
  (ITALIAN) PARSLEY LEAVES,
  ROUGHLY CHOPPED
1 HANDFUL MINT LEAVES,
  ROUGHLY CHOPPED
2 TEASPOONS SUMAC
SEA SALT AND FRESHLY GROUND
  BLACK PEPPER
EXTRA ½ TEASPOON SUMAC, FOR
  SERVING

DRESSING
125 ML (½ CUP) OLIVE OIL
80 ML (⅓ CUP) LEMON JUICE
1 TABLESPOON POMEGRANATE
  MOLASSES
1½ TEASPOONS SALT
½ TEASPOON SUGAR

Preheat the oven to 170°C (325°F/Gas 3).

Using a pastry brush, paint the bread with the olive oil, place on a baking tray and bake until golden brown, about 10 minutes. Allow to cool, then break into pieces.

To make the dressing, combine all ingredients in a bowl or shake in a jar.

Place all the prepared vegetables and herbs in a salad bowl. Sprinkle with the sumac and enough of the dressing to coat the leaves. Mix well. Add the bread and gently toss. Taste for seasoning and add more salt and pepper if needed. Sprinkle with the extra sumac to serve.

Serves 8

My mother entertained generously, but cooking wasn't her first love. It was my Australian mother-in-law who really ignited my passion for cooking.

On a trip home to London many years ago, my cousin Lyn gave me a recipe for florentine biscuits, which I'd never seen before. I had my second baby and started making them for cafés, pushing the pram around Bondi to make deliveries. My repertoire expanded to cakes, and culminated in the opening of Cuisine in 1997 with my friend and business partner, Anne. Anne retired and then Pearl became my business partner. Twenty-five years later, we sold the business.

I still love to cook and entertain, with a full house every Friday night. My daughters are great cooks, and my four-year-old grandson loves to potter with me in the kitchen. He's a grandmother's delight – even when I discover he has cracked eggs into the kitchen drawer!

JACK SAGES, TANYA BEVERLEY AND NILLY BERGER

FATHER, DAUGHTER AND NIECE

Jack

Jack Sages was the sixth generation of his family to be born in Turkey, after his ancestors were driven out of Spain during the Spanish Inquisition. He lived in Sydney with his wife and companion of 55 years, artist Jenny Sages, until he passed away in 2010.

Jack's mother and sister Rachel were very good in the kitchen. Jack started cooking because he was hungry; Jenny didn't cook!

Jack often said that he had no qualifications as a cook, but he had a lot of inside know-how because of his closeness to his mother. He grew to love being in the kitchen. He spoke with delight about visiting Turkey, going out early in the morning and seeing the local shopkeepers arranging their fruit for the day, displaying them with love and attention.

This passion for cooking has been handed down to his daughter Tanya and grandchildren; Jack's memory lives on in the recipes and stories he left behind.

Tanya

My mother is an extremely talented artist but cooking has never been her thing. Luckily my father had a true passion for cooking. We loved sharing recipes and sampling each other's dishes. I miss him and his albondigas *(Spanish meatballs) very much.*

My grandmothers were wonderful cooks. Bubbie (my mother's mum) made delicious matzo ball soup, borscht, and chicken kotletki *(chicken rissoles). Whenever I was sick she prepared the best medicine: 'goggle moggle', a warm eggnog drink. Though my dad's mother died before I was born, her amazing recipes have lived on through him and Aunty Rachel.*

I live with my husband in rural New South Wales. Cooking is one of the reasons I fell in love with him. The first night we met, he made a delicious satay chicken and that was it, I was in love. He and his mother, Jan, inspired me to become a better cook.

Nilly

My parents, Rachel and Chaim Shalom, both immigrated to Israel as children from Turkey in the 1930s. As newlyweds they lived in a small apartment with my grandparents. Cooking and eating were a big part of their lives and I grew up the happy recipient of delicious and plentiful food. We lived in Brazil for six years before joining my uncle Jack and grandparents in Sydney.

Even though my love of good food began early in life, I was never allowed to help my mother in the kitchen. My own cooking began when I married into the Berger family, which owns Sydney's iconic Gelato Bar. Since 1958 it has been a home away from home for the Eastern European community. Australians love its continental food; people still ogle its lavish displays of cakes and biscuits. Now our daughters have a passion for cooking and eating, having grown up in our combined Sephardi and Hungarian kitchen.

This is a traditional Turkish sweet often sold wrapped in cellophane. It is a lovely way to finish a meal with a cup of sweetened fresh mint tea.

Sesame sweet

250 G (9 OZ/2 CUPS) SESAME SEEDS
250 G (9 OZ/1 CUP PLUS 1 TABLESPOON)
   SUGAR
1 TABLESPOON HONEY

Place a large sheet of baking paper, about 60 x 30 cm (24 x 12 inches), on a work surface or chopping board.

Toast the sesame seeds in a frying pan over low heat until golden, taking care not to burn them.

Put the sugar and honey in a heavy-based non-stick saucepan and cook over medium heat until the sugar is dissolved, stirring constantly with a wooden spoon. Boil for several minutes until the mixture is a rich golden colour. Add the sesame seeds and stir well.

Carefully pour the hot mixture onto the baking paper, then cover immediately with another sheet of baking paper. Working quickly, use a rolling pin to firmly roll out the sesame mixture to about 5 mm (¼ inch) thick. Cut immediately into diamond shapes or leave whole till cool, then break into shards.

Store in an airtight container for up to one week.

Makes a 60 x 30 cm (24 x 12 inch) slab

These leek and beef patties are from my mother and Jack Sages' sister, Rachel, who is still to this day an outstanding cook. For a vegetarian version, substitute two potatoes, boiled and mashed, for the beef mince.

Prassa (leek patties)

1 KG (2 LB 4 OZ) LEEKS, WASHED
   AND TRIMMED
300 G (10½ OZ) MINCED (GROUND)
   BEEF
3 EGGS, LIGHTLY WHISKED
40 G (⅓ CUP) FINE MATZO MEAL OR
   DRY BREADCRUMBS
SEA SALT AND FRESHLY GROUND
   BLACK PEPPER
60 ML (¼ CUP) VEGETABLE OIL
2 TABLESPOONS OLIVE OIL
2 TABLESPOONS TOMATO PASTE
   (CONCENTRATED PURÉE)
185 ML (¾ CUP) WATER

Using only the white part and some of the pale green section, finely chop the leeks or process in a food processor until quite fine, but not a purée.

Bring a saucepan of water to the boil, add the leek and simmer until soft, about 5 minutes. Drain well and squeeze out any remaining liquid with your hands.

Place the beef, eggs and matzo meal or breadcrumbs in a bowl and add the leeks. Mix well and season generously with salt and pepper. Shape into patties.

Heat the vegetable oil in a large frying pan and shallow-fry the patties in batches, turning, until dark golden. Drain on paper towel.

Once the patties have all been cooked, discard the oil and wipe out the pan with paper towel. Return the pan to the heat with the olive oil, then add the tomato paste and water and mix until combined. Bring to a simmer and place all the patties in the sauce. Cover and cook for a few minutes on each side, turning once, until the patties are cooked through and the tomato sauce has been absorbed.

Makes 20 patties

These are a wonderful and impressive pastry to serve as a light meal, but are so simple to make. Serve hot alongside a simple green salad for lunch. It's best to take the filo out of the fridge at least 2 hours before making to allow the coils to be rolled more easily.

Spinach and feta coils

8–10 SHEETS FILO PASTRY

1 BUNCH ENGLISH SPINACH, ABOUT 180 G (6½ OZ) LEAVES

250 G (9 OZ) FETA CHEESE

100 G (3½ OZ) PECORINO CHEESE, GRATED

100 G (3½ OZ) PARMESAN CHEESE, GRATED

1 TABLESPOON PLAIN (ALL-PURPOSE) FLOUR

2 EGGS

100 G (3½ OZ) BUTTER, MELTED

100 ML (SCANT ½ CUP) VEGETABLE OIL

1 EGG, LIGHTLY BEATEN, FOR GLAZING

SESAME SEEDS

Take the filo pastry out of the fridge at least 2 hours before starting the recipe to minimise cracking when shaping the coils.

Preheat the oven to 200°C (400°F/Gas 6). Line two baking trays.

Wash the spinach, remove and discard the large stems and chop the leaves. Blanch in boiling water, then drain thoroughly. Leave to cool slightly, then squeeze out as much excess water as possible. The cooked spinach should weigh about 85 g (3 oz).

Crumble the feta into a bowl, add the other cheeses, flour, eggs and spinach and mix well.

Combine the melted butter and oil in a bowl.

Place 1 sheet of the filo in front of you vertically on the benchtop. Cover the remaining sheets with a damp cloth. Lightly brush the butter mixture over the filo sheet, ensuring the entire surface is covered. Make a 4 cm (1½ inch) fold at the short end of the pastry sheet, then spread a 2 cm (¾ inch) thick layer of the spinach filling over this fold from left to right, leaving about 2 cm (¾ inch) space at both ends.

Fold both the long sides of the pastry inwards to prevent leakage, then roll the pastry up from the bottom to the top to make a cylinder. Wrap the cylinder into a coil shape and place on a prepared tray. Repeat the process with the remaining filling and filo sheets until you have 8–10 coils. Brush the tops with beaten egg and sprinkle over the sesame seeds. Bake for 25–30 minutes until golden brown. Use a paper towel to remove any excess oil before serving.

Serves 8–10

Photos on page 56–7

{Spinach and feta coils}

Quite a few of my friends are gluten intolerant, so I'm always looking for delicious gluten-free recipes. This recipe is an adaptation of a wonderful Nigella Lawson cake; the oranges make it deliciously moist and decadent but because it has no butter or oil It's not heavy. I love making this cake; it never fails and I can always rely on it to impress.

Chocolate orange cake

3 SMALL THIN-SKINNED ORANGES
300 G (2 CUPS) WHOLE ALMONDS, TOASTED
9 EGGS
2¼ TEASPOONS BAKING POWDER
400 G (14 OZ/1¾ CUPS) RAW (DEMERARA) SUGAR
100 G (3½ OZ/1 CUP) BEST-QUALITY COCOA POWDER

GANACHE
360 G (12¾ OZ) BEST-QUALITY DARK CHOCOLATE, CHOPPED
250 ML (1 CUP) PURE CREAM (35% FAT)

Preheat the oven to 180°C (350°F/Gas 4). Grease and line a 28 cm (11 inch) springform cake tin.

Place the oranges in a saucepan and cover with water. Bring to the boil, then turn down to a simmer for 2 hours, turning occasionally. Remove from the cooking liquid and cool.

In the meantime, grind the almonds in a food processor until fine. Set aside.

When the oranges are cool, cut into quarters, remove any pips and weigh out 560 g (1 lb 4¼ oz). (The rest can be discarded.) Pulp the cooked orange in the food processor until just smooth. Add the ground almonds and all the other ingredients and process until just combined, scraping down the side of the bowl with a spatula every now and then.

Pour the mixture into the prepared tin and bake for 1 hour, or until golden and a skewer inserted in the cake comes out clean, bearing in mind it is a moist cake.

Allow to cool in the tin.

Make the ganache once the cake is cool. Put the chocolate in a heatproof bowl. Heat the cream to almost boiling point, then pour over the chocolate and stir until smooth. Leave to cool slightly and then whisk for a few minutes until thick but still able to be spread. Spread over the cake and allow to set.

Serves 10–12

COLETTE LEVY

Growing up in Cairo was glorious; there were boisterous family meals, always served by a maid but prepared by my mother before she went out to play cards. She promised to teach me how to cook all the family recipes once I married; however, during the Suez Crisis in 1956, my fiancé, Ray, was expelled and I was given permission to leave with him. We left with only a few days' notice and consequently I didn't have all those important cooking lessons until many years later.

We arrived in London as refugees. The Jewish community at the Spanish Portuguese Synagogue arranged our wedding; I knew none of the guests. Three years later, we made our way to Adelaide.

After many years I was able to take my two daughters to Milan to meet their grandmother, Nona Angele, where I could at last cook with her and learn her recipes. I loved the comforting smell of all the spices in her kitchen and my daughters fondly remember family lunches of ful medames (an Egyptian dish of mashed and cooked broad beans), eaten with homemade pita bread, boiled egg and tahini.

Today I enjoy making the sweets my grandchildren love, and I send food parcels to them in Melbourne and Sydney, each with their favourites.

I have been making this basboussa recipe for nearly 40 years and it is my daughters' favourite. I love the sweet syrupy flavour and the crunch from the almonds. It is important to use fine semolina to get the right texture. Because we are more health conscious these days, I sometimes reduce the butter or sugar content, but I am a believer that everything in moderation is fine, so just enjoy.

Basboussa

360 G (12¾ oz/2 cups) **FINE SEMOLINA**
220 G (7¾ oz/1 cup) **SUGAR**
2¼ TEASPOONS BAKING POWDER
250 G (9 oz) **UNSALTED BUTTER, MELTED**
¼ TEASPOON VANILLA SUGAR
250 ML (1 cup) **MILK**
25 BLANCHED ALMONDS

SYRUP

440 G (2 cups) **SUGAR**
250 ML (1 cup) **WATER**
JUICE OF ½ LEMON
¼ TEASPOON VANILLA EXTRACT

Combine the semolina with the sugar, baking powder, melted butter, vanilla sugar and ½ a cup of the milk. Allow the mixture to stand and swell for 30 minutes.

Preheat the oven to 180°C (350°F/Gas 4). You will need a rectangular baking tin, approximately 27 x 18 x 3 cm (10¾ x 7 x 1¼ inches). Line the base with baking paper, leaving an overhang on both sides so the basboussa is easy to remove.

Add the remaining milk to the semolina mixture and stir to combine. Pour into the prepared tin and bake for 20–25 minutes, or until just golden and slightly set – you must be able to cut it at this stage. Remove from the oven and make 3–4 cm (1¼–1½ inch) slices across the tin, and then diagonally from corner to corner to create diamond shapes. Press an almond, pointy side up, into each diamond.

Combine all the syrup ingredients together in a saucepan and simmer until the sugar is dissolved. Continue to boil until the liquid thickens and is tacky, about 10 minutes.

Return the basboussa to the oven and bake for a further 10 minutes until golden. Remove from the oven, spoon the cooled syrup over the hot basboussa, then return to the oven for a further 10 minutes.

Turn the oven off, leaving the basboussa in for a further 30 minutes. Remove from the tin and cut into diamonds to serve. Store in an airtight container for up to 3 weeks.

Makes approximately 25 pieces

My mum used to make these delicious, buttery fingers for the small home-baking business she started when we first moved to Australia. An easy recipe that never fails, it is one of my kids' favourites. They always fight over the edges left in the tin – if I don't eat them first! – Lauren Fink

Granny's shortbread

175 G (6 OZ) UNSALTED BUTTER, CHOPPED, AT ROOM TEMPERATURE

45 G (1½ OZ) CORNFLOUR (CORNSTARCH)

225 G (8 OZ/1½ CUPS) PLAIN (ALL-PURPOSE) FLOUR

90 G (3¼ OZ) CASTER (SUPERFINE) SUGAR, PLUS EXTRA FOR SPRINKLING

Preheat the oven to 150°C (300°F/Gas 2). Grease a 30 x 20 cm (12 x 8 inch) baking tin.

Process all the ingredients in a food processor until you have a slightly crumbly dough.

Tip the dough into the prepared tin and spread out evenly, pressing it with your fingers or a flat spatula until level. Prick all over with a fork. Bake until golden on the edges, about 1 hour.

Remove from the oven and, while still in the tin, immediately cut into fingers with a sharp knife. Leave in the tin until cool. Sprinkle with the extra caster sugar and remove from the tin to serve.

Makes 24–30 shortbread

Read Lauren's story on page 15

Everyday

What's to eat? The never-ending question. I am always searching for inspiration for anything from weeknight dinners to easy weekend brunches. I'm looking for doable recipes with simple but delicious flavours that will keep my family and friends happy. A one-pot dish like a beef Bourguigon that can be made in the morning and served that night makes my day run smoothly.

Jacqui ♡

Recipes

{Beef and potato pie}

JACQUI ISRAEL

My love for breakfast spurred me on to find the best bircher muesli in Sydney, but I always liked a bit of this one and a bit of that. So I decided to make up my own, inspired by David Cullen's recipe from the wonderful Sugar Café some years ago. After testing, changing, adding new ingredients, putting in more of some things and less of others, I finally perfected The Bircher.

Bircher muesli

120 G (1 CUP) ROLLED (PORRIDGE)
   OATS

375 ML (1½ CUPS) APPLE JUICE

45 G (¼ CUP) PITTED DRIED DATES,
   CHOPPED

60 G (⅓ CUP) DRIED APRICOTS,
   CHOPPED

1 RED APPLE, PEELED, CORED AND
   GRATED

175 G (6 OZ/¾ CUP) GREEK-STYLE
   YOGHURT

2 TABLESPOONS RAW OR ROASTED
   BUCKWHEAT

2 TABLESPOONS LINSEEDS
   (FLAXSEEDS)

35 G (¼ CUP) SUNFLOWER SEEDS

40 G (⅓ CUP) SLIVERED ALMONDS,
   TOASTED

Start this recipe a day before serving.

Soak the oats in the apple juice in a ceramic or glass bowl and leave overnight (in the refrigerator), covered with plastic wrap.

The next day, add all the remaining ingredients, except the almonds, and mix together.

Sprinkle the almonds on top just before serving.

Serves 8–10

Read Jacqui's story on page 16

This soup is an adaptation of a good friend's recipe. She originally got it from a neighbour, and now I am the one to pass it on. It is simple, delicious and always works out perfectly.

Zucchini, pea and mint soup

2–3 LEEKS (350 G/12 OZ), WHITE
  PART ONLY, SLICED
2 TABLESPOONS OLIVE OIL
8–10 ZUCCHINIS (1 KG/2 LB 4 OZ)
  (COURGETTES), SLICED
3 CUPS (500 G/1 LB 2 OZ) PEAS
1.5 LITRES (6 CUPS) CHICKEN OR
  VEGETABLE STOCK
1 BUNCH MINT, LEAVES ONLY
SEA SALT AND FRESHLY GROUND
  BLACK PEPPER

In a large saucepan over medium heat, fry the leek in the olive oil until soft, then add the zucchini and continue to cook until wilted and soft. Add the peas and enough stock to cover, then simmer until all the vegetables are cooked through, about 30 minutes.

Take off the heat and allow to cool slightly, then add the mint leaves and blend. Season generously with salt and pepper.

Serves 8–10

I've lived in Sydney all my life. In fact, I live in the same suburb I grew up in. I am first-generation Australian; my Polish mother and Hungarian father both survived the war and were lucky enough to make Australia home. My mother was a smart businesswoman with little interest in cooking. Growing up with the same school lunch for twelve years, I was determined to become a good cook and started learning when I got married, inspired by my talented sister-in-law and friends.

I have lovely memories of sitting around my grandparents' tiny kitchen table. Whatever my grandmother served, my grandfather thought he was eating in a Michelin-star restaurant. Today I am a proud gatherer of recipes, with cookbooks as my bedtime reading. I still laugh at the time I bumped into Bill Granger. After telling him how I loved his new cookbook and read it each night before going to sleep, my husband sheepishly added, 'Sometimes I wish I were your cookbook!'

These days my passion for cooking is shared by my kids. It gives me the greatest nachas, although they haven't quite mastered the cleaning up.

ANTONIA HARALAMBIS AND AMBER SCHWARZ

SISTERS

Antonia

I have always been curious about food and loved the way food dominated our household growing up. An inordinate amount of time was spent discussing innovative dishes, newly discovered ingredients and what was in season. My grandmother was a wonderful cook and was famous among her friends for her dinner parties. I was also inspired by our Spanish housekeeper who made mouth-watering churros and the most flavoursome gazpacho, perfect for a dieting teenager!

I started playing around with food on a more professional level with a few catering jobs, then as a breakfast chef at a Woollahra café. This experience, using food in a fresh, innovative, no-fuss style, heavily influenced the way I would cook for family and friends in later years. I went to the Prue Leith Cooking School in London, then did work experience at Marco Pierre White's restaurant Harvey's – a real eye-opener for a 21-year-old.

Today I enjoy cooking as a passion, rather than a profession. The kitchen is where I go for meditation; it is through the creative process of cooking I find peace of mind.

Amber

My family originates from all over Europe; my mother's side is German and Dutch, and my father's, Lithuanian and Russian. We were a very close-knit family, and my mother had the gift of my nana, her mother, to help raise us.

The kitchen table was always the centre of our house. My mother cooked well and loved exposing us to adult food and flavours. My nana too was a culinary queen; her house excited my senses with different flavours and smells and the constant chatter that surrounded her long, immaculately set dining table. I believe one's generosity of spirit and the act of giving can be reflected in cooking and sharing food with family and friends. I would like to think I inherited that quality from both of them.

When I married, I could not even boil an egg. After several years in New York I returned to Sydney and began taking regular cooking classes at Accoutrement with Antonia and my mother. A wonderful tradition was born, and still to this day the three of us (now all accomplished cooks) attend monthly classes together. I am a proudly health-conscious cook and hope to pass this on to my children, both of whom appreciate and enjoy good food.

I created this dish many years ago when I was an in-house chef for a wonderful Jewish accounting firm in London. This slow-roasted tomato sauce is one of the most tempting options for non-meat eaters I developed, with intense, delicious flavour from the garlic, capers, anchovies and olives. It freezes well and like many dishes, tastes even better the next day.

Slow-roasted tomato sauce for spaghetti

80 ML (⅓ CUP) EXTRA VIRGIN OLIVE
  OIL
2 KG (4 LB 8 OZ) VERY RIPE
  TOMATOES, CUT INTO 1 CM
  (½ INCH) SLICES
2 RED ONIONS, SLICED
2 CLOVES GARLIC, CRUSHED
50 G (¼ CUP) SALTED BABY CAPERS,
  WELL RINSED AND DRAINED
8 ANCHOVY FILLETS, EACH CUT
  INTO 3
120 G (¾ CUP) PITTED KALAMATA
  OLIVES
FRESHLY GROUND BLACK PEPPER
SEA SALT
1 TABLESPOON TOMATO PASTE
  (CONCENTRATED PURÉE)
500 G (1 LB 2 OZ) SPAGHETTI
40 G (½ CUP) GRATED PARMESAN
  CHEESE
½ BUNCH FLAT-LEAF (Italian)
  PARSLEY, CHOPPED
¼ BUNCH BASIL, LEAVES
  SHREDDED

GARNISH
40 G (½ CUP) TOASTED PINE NUTS
1 HANDFUL FLAT-LEAF (Italian)
  PARSLEY, CHOPPED
EXTRA PARMESAN CHEESE

Preheat the oven to 200°C (400°F/Gas 6).

Use two large roasting dishes (non-stick if possible) to layer the ingredients. Start with a splash of the olive oil, then divide the tomato, onion, garlic, capers and anchovies between each dish, add another splash of oil and scatter on the olives and pepper. Finish with another splash of olive oil.

Place the dishes in the oven, then turn the temperature down to 170°C (325°F/Gas 3). Roast for about 1½–2 hours, or until soft and a little caramelised, but not so that all of the liquid has evaporated. Turn the mixture every 20 minutes or so to avoid burning. When cooked, combine the contents of both dishes, taste for seasoning and add the tomato paste. Add salt sparingly, as the capers, anchovies and olives will all provide saltiness.

Cook the spaghetti in plenty of salted boiling water, drain, reserving ¼ cup of the pasta water.

In a large bowl, mix the cooked pasta with the roasted tomato sauce and parmesan, adding some of the extra cooking liquid if necessary. Mix in the parsley, basil and a dash of extra virgin olive oil. Transfer to a large platter. Scatter the pine nuts and parsley on top and serve hot or at room temperature with extra parmesan cheese.

Makes 5 cups pasta sauce
Serves 6

My cooking over the years has been deeply influenced by a healthy lifestyle and the importance of integrity in what we eat. Quality of ingredients and knowing where they come from is very important to me so I know exactly what I am feeding my family. This simple fish recipe reflects my attitude – it has no added fat and is quick and easy to prepare. I like to substitute tamari for the soy.

Maple and soy ocean trout

1 SIDE OCEAN TROUT, WEIGHING ABOUT 1 KG (2 LB 4 OZ), SKINNED AND PIN-BONED

185 ML (¾ CUP) SOY SAUCE

185 ML (¾ CUP) PURE MAPLE SYRUP

1½ TABLESPOONS FINELY GRATED FRESH GINGER

1½ TABLESPOONS LIME JUICE

2 TABLESPOONS TOASTED SESAME SEEDS, FOR SERVING

LIME WEDGES, FOR SERVING

Start this recipe the day before serving.

Lay the fish in a deep ceramic or other non-reactive ovenproof dish. Mix the soy sauce, maple syrup, ginger and lime juice in a small bowl, then pour over so that the fish is covered with the liquid. Cover with plastic wrap and refrigerate for 24 hours, turning once.

Take the marinated fish out of the fridge 2 hours before cooking to bring to room temperature.

Preheat the oven to 200°C (400°F/Gas 6).

Roast the fish in the marinade, uncovered, for 15 minutes (rare) to 30 minutes (well done), or until cooked to your liking. Remove from the oven and rest for the same amount of time as the cooking, remembering that it will continue to cook.

Remove the fish from the sauce, cover and set aside. Pour the sauce through a sieve into a small saucepan. Simmer on the stove to reduce and thicken.

Serve the fish on a platter, drizzle with the sauce, and garnish with the toasted sesame seeds and lime wedges. Accompany with jasmine rice and steamed green vegetables tossed with sesame oil, if desired.

Serves 6–8, depending on size of fish

I love learning new recipes, especially from my Greek mother-in-law, Maria. She made these meatballs for my children when they were toddlers. They are great for school lunchboxes, for kids' or adult parties, or as part of a larger family buffet meal. The meatballs are so delicious and can be served warm or at room temperature. Maria's trick in making them fabulously light is a good pinch of baking powder and rolling them in self-raising flour instead of plain flour.

Maria's keftethes (Greek meatballs)

250 G (9 OZ/ABOUT ½ LOAF) STALE SOURDOUGH BREAD, CRUSTS REMOVED

1 KG (2 LB 4 OZ) MINCED (GROUND) BEEF

2 EGGS, BEATEN

2 BROWN ONIONS, GRATED

½ TEASPOON PAPRIKA

½ TEASPOON FRESHLY GRATED NUTMEG

1 BUNCH FLAT-LEAF (ITALIAN) PARSLEY, FINELY CHOPPED

3 CLOVES GARLIC, CRUSHED

½ TEASPOON BAKING POWDER

2 TEASPOONS LEMON JUICE

80 ML (⅓ CUP) OLIVE OIL

SEA SALT AND FRESHLY GROUND BLACK PEPPER

150 G (1 CUP) SELF-RAISING FLOUR

VEGETABLE OIL, FOR FRYING

Cover the bread in water for a few minutes. Drain and squeeze well, then grate into a large bowl. Add the beef, eggs, onion, paprika, nutmeg, parsley, garlic, baking powder, lemon juice and oil. Combine well with your hands and season generously with salt and pepper to taste. Cover and refrigerate for at least 1 hour.

Scatter the flour on a small tray. Prepare a small bowl with water. Heat the vegetable oil in a large frying pan over medium heat. With wet hands, shape the meat mixture into golf ball-sized meatballs. Roll them in the flour and fry immediately, in batches, turning the heat down if they brown too quickly. Remove and drain on paper towel. Keep warm until ready to serve.

Makes approximately 70 meatballs

These have always been my mother-in-law Yvonne's staple for Shabbat and yomtov dinners. I never thought to recreate them as there was no written recipe and she made them perfectly. Inspired by the Monday Morning Cooking Club, I watched Yvonne carefully and now my children request them for all their birthday Shabbat dinners. I still get nervous when Yvonne comes for dinner and sit there wondering, are they as good as hers? – Lauren Fink

Nanna's chicken balls

125 ML (½ CUP) VEGETABLE OIL

8 ONIONS, CHOPPED

1 KG (2 LB 4 OZ) MINCED (GROUND)
    CHICKEN THIGH

1 EGG

2 TABLESPOONS TOMATO PASTE
    (CONCENTRATED PURÉE)

2 TABLESPOONS TOMATO SAUCE
    (KETCHUP)

70 G (½ CUP) DRY BREADCRUMBS

80 ML (⅓ CUP) WATER

SEA SALT AND FRESHLY GROUND
    BLACK PEPPER

SAUCE

2 x 400 G (14 OZ) TINS DICED
    ITALIAN TOMATOES

300 ML TOMATO PASSATA (PURÉED
    TOMATOES)

2 TABLESPOONS TOMATO PASTE
    (CONCENTRATED PURÉE)

60 ML (¼ CUP) WATER

1 x 400 G (14 OZ) TIN CONDENSED
    TOMATO SOUP

Heat the oil in a wide-based flameproof casserole dish or saucepan over medium–high heat and fry the onion until golden brown. Transfer three-quarters of the fried onions to a large bowl. Set aside to cool slightly.

To make the chicken mixture, combine the chicken, egg, tomato paste, tomato sauce, breadcrumbs, water and salt and pepper with the cooled onions in the bowl. Mix well. Refrigerate for 30 minutes.

To make the sauce, place all the ingredients in the flameproof dish or pan with the remaining fried onions. Bring to the boil, then reduce the heat to a simmer and cook for 10 minutes.

Wet your hands and form the chicken mixture into golf ball-sized balls. Working quickly, place the balls in the sauce, shaking the pot to move them around. Do not use a spoon until they become more firm. Continue adding the chicken balls until all the mixture has been used. Cover and simmer for 40 minutes, stirring occasionally.

Serve with risoni or short pasta.

Serves 8–10

Read Lauren's story on page 15

A simple dish of fresh fish with spices and a knob of butter served on top of nutty burghul. This is traditionally called 'Adana' snapper and is made in a clay pot.

Clay pot snapper with burghul pilaf

750 G (1 LB 10 OZ/ ABOUT 4 LARGE)
   SNAPPER FILLETS, SKIN OFF
1½ TABLESPOONS ATA'S SPICE
   MIX: EQUAL QUANTITIES
   GROUND TURMERIC, SWEET
   PAPRIKA, HOT PAPRIKA, CUMIN,
   BAHARAT, CHILLI (OPTIONAL)
½ BUNCH FLAT-LEAF (ITALIAN)
   PARSLEY, LEAVES ONLY
   ROUGHLY CHOPPED
50 G (1¾ OZ) BUTTER, CHOPPED
SEA SALT
1 LEMON, SLICED
1 TABLESPOON OLIVE OIL
CHOPPED FRESH CHILLI OR
   PICKLED PEPPERS, FOR SERVING

BURGHUL PILAF

30 G (1 OZ) BUTTER
40 G (¼ CUP) TURKISH SOUP
   NOODLES OR CRUSHED FINE
   VERMICELLI
200 G (1 HEAPED CUP) MEDIUM
   COARSE BURGHUL (BULGUR)
375 ML (1½ CUPS) BOILING WATER
1 SMALL HANDFUL FLAT-LEAF
   (ITALIAN) PARSLEY LEAVES,
   ROUGHLY CHOPPED

You will need a clay pot or a wide flat ovenproof dish.

Toss the fish with the spice mix, three-quarters of the parsley leaves and the butter and place in the clay pot or dish. Leave to marinate at room temperature for 30 minutes.

Preheat the oven to 210°C (410°F/Gas 6–7).

Season the fish generously with salt, top with the lemon slices and drizzle with the olive oil. Cover with foil or a lid and roast for 20 minutes. Remove the cover and return to the oven for 5 minutes, or until the fish is just cooked through.

Meanwhile, to make the burghul pilaf, melt the butter in a frying pan over medium heat. Add the noodles and toss, then add the burghul and cook in the butter for a minute. Add 1 cup of the water and stir. Cover with a lid, turn the heat down and cook for 5 minutes until the burghul softens and the water is absorbed. Add the remaining water, stir, cover with the lid and cook for a few minutes until the water is absorbed. If the burghul is not cooked once all the water has been absorbed, add a little more water and steam until just cooked. Add the parsley and season with salt.

Garnish the fish with the remaining parsley and serve with the burghul pilaf and the chilli on the side.

Serves 4

Read Ata's story on page 112

My mother often makes this chicken for a quick Sunday night dinner with the family. She serves it with a delicious crisp green salad and the best ever roasted potatoes with duck fat. She always whips together something so simple and easy but so delicious, you would think she had slaved away in the kitchen all day.

Chicken with olives and capers

1 CHICKEN, JOINTED, OR
  4 CHICKEN MARYLANDS (LEG QUARTERS)
50 G (¼ CUP) SALTED BABY CAPERS, WELL RINSED AND DRAINED
75 G (½ CUP) PITTED KALAMATA OLIVES, HALVED
2 CLOVES GARLIC, UNPEELED
250 ML (1 CUP) WHITE WINE
1 TABLESPOON OLIVE OIL
3 THYME SPRIGS
FRESHLY GROUND BLACK PEPPER

Preheat the oven to 200°C (400°F/Gas 6).

Place the chicken pieces in an oiled roasting dish, then scatter the capers, olives and garlic on top. Pour the wine and olive oil over the chicken, then scatter on the thyme and season generously with pepper.

Roast for 45 minutes to 1 hour, or until the chicken is golden and the juices run clear when pierced with a knife. If the chicken is not browned enough, turn the oven to the hottest setting for the last 5 minutes.

Serves 4

I grew up surrounded by my mother and aunties always talking about new recipes and ideas on what to make that night for dinner, or planning a sumptuous feast for one of the yomtovs. Even though my mum came to Australia from Poland when she was only thirteen years old, not speaking a word of English, and my dad came from Israel, we do not really cook any dishes from their heritage. Mum's only nod to their culinary backgrounds was to use lots of chilli for my spice-crazy dad.

Rather, Mum instilled in my sister and me a love of cooking with fresh, healthy ingredients inspired by what is around us. I often asked to skip school so I could stay home and cook. Sometimes we would head off to a food market far away or go to the mountains and pick mushrooms.

My husband is a sixth-generation Australian whose family are mad chocoholics and they have somewhat corrupted our healthy ways. There 'must' be dessert and it 'must' feature chocolate.

Dad always says that Mum has passed her special touch on to me. I hope I can pass it on to my children.

Pollo con salsa is a classic Argentinian dish still found in many restaurants today. My mother's recipe fills the house with the delicious smell of garlic and tomatoes. It is the perfect winter dish, served with rice, pasta, couscous or simply on its own. I love to bring it to the table in the pot I make it in, tempting my guests with its rich vibrant colour and aroma.

Pollo con salsa

2 TABLESPOONS OLIVE OIL

1 LARGE RED ONION, THINLY
  SLICED

1 LARGE RED CAPSICUM (PEPPER),
  THINLY SLICED

6 CLOVES GARLIC, CRUSHED, OR
  TO TASTE

8 SKINLESS CHICKEN THIGH
  FILLETS (OR DRUMSTICKS)

500 ML (2 CUPS) CHICKEN STOCK

1 X 400 G (14 OZ) TIN DICED
  ITALIAN TOMATOES

SEA SALT AND FRESHLY GROUND
  BLACK PEPPER

1 LARGE HANDFUL FLAT-LEAF
  (ITALIAN) PARSLEY, ROUGHLY
  CHOPPED

You will need a large deep frying pan with a lid. In the pan, heat the oil, add the onion and fry over a medium heat for 10 minutes, or until soft. Add the capsicum and garlic and fry for another 5 minutes until soft. Remove from the pan and set aside. Add the chicken pieces to the pan and brown well on each side.

Return the onion mix to the chicken in the pan and add the stock. Cover with the lid and cook over a low heat for 30 minutes, or until just tender. Stir in the tomatoes and season with salt and pepper. Sprinkle the parsley on top and cook, uncovered, for a further 15 minutes, or until done.

Serves 4

While other kids around me were eating their sausage rolls and meat pies, I grew up with creamed corn empanadas, homemade ñoquis (similar to gnocchi) and pastel de papa (Argentinian shepherd's pie). My South American mother spent a lot of time preparing these delicious treats, and it was no surprise that I loved cooking from an early age.

I carried her recipes with me when my husband and I moved to Canberra almost a decade ago, and have since cooked them for a growing Jewish community. The first time we sat down to a communal Seder, I turned to my husband and said, 'Remind me, if we're here again next year, to cook for the Seder!' Sure enough, the year after, seven months pregnant with twins, I was in our shul's kitchen preparing 120 kneidlach.

Today my mother calls our house 'la casa del pueblo' (the village house), because my kitchen has become a revolving door through which many friends come and go, to our great delight.

My wonderful Latvian mother-in-law is also a fabulous cook. So we enjoy the best of both worlds, the melting pot of life.

NATALIE TOPPER AND ADAM LOPATA

SISTER AND BROTHER

Natalie

For some, cooking is a chore, but for me it has always been a joyful creative outlet. The kitchen is my happy place and for as long as I can remember I have been obsessed with food.

I am second-generation Australian, born and raised in Sydney. I grew up in a house filled with children laughing and endless food being served. My mother, Bessie, has always been a huge source of inspiration for me. She can magically produce sensational last-minute meals.

You will always find me sitting on the couch, in bed or in front of the TV reading cookbooks. Food is a focus in my family: my mother-in-law, Sandra, whips up meals any chef would be proud of, and my brother, Adam, is always discussing new food ideas for his café in Double Bay.

My husband and I have three young children and we sit together each night at the dinner table and discuss our day. Food unites us. I am so pleased that our kids are now asking to help me in the kitchen and really hope that this is the start of a bond that will last forever.

Adam

My earliest memories are standing in the kitchen, watching my mum plan and cook for Shabbat dinners and parties with great ease. Every Sunday morning was spent with Dad at Starks, the kosher store in Bondi, stocking up on bagels, salmon, herring and chopped egg.

Coming from an Eastern European background, we always had salami, cheeses, liver and other delicacies in the fridge. The first time my mum packed a cheese and vegemite sandwich in my lunchbox, I rushed to call her from the school office, shocked by the mistake she had made. She was only trying to give me what she had longed for as a kid, an Aussie lunch. Thankfully, we were soon back to schnitzel sandwiches.

We ate out often, and I soon developed a passion for food and restaurants. From a young age I knew I wanted to work in the industry. I have owned a number of cafés, and food is always my focus. Even when travelling, I'm on the lookout for new ideas and combinations to introduce at my current location in Double Bay, Café Arno, where the specials change constantly to showcase Sydney's wonderful fresh produce.

I often have families over for dinner at the last minute and so my favourite recipes are those that are very easy and quick to prepare from ingredients found in every pantry. This is a perfect marinade for even the fussiest of eaters, and can be used for chicken, beef and different cuts of lamb. It can be made the night before to let the flavour develop or at the very last minute if you have run out of time.

Marinated lamb cutlets

16 LAMB CUTLETS, FRENCH TRIMMED

MARINADE
80 ML (⅓ CUP) OLIVE OIL
2 TABLESPOONS DIJON MUSTARD
1 TABLESPOON CHOPPED FLAT-LEAF (ITALIAN) PARSLEY
2 TABLESPOONS SOY SAUCE
6 CLOVES GARLIC, CRUSHED
FRESHLY GROUND BLACK PEPPER

Combine all the marinade ingredients in a bowl and mix well.

Coat the cutlets in the marinade and refrigerate for 2 hours or overnight. Heat a barbecue or ridged grill pan to very hot, then cook the cutlets for 2–3 minutes on each side for medium, or to your liking.

Serves 6–8

These potatoes are always a winner – with both adults and children of all ages. They can be prepared beforehand and placed in the oven later on in the evening. You can add various herbs (such as rosemary) for those with a more sophisticated palate. I also like that minimal oil is required.

Smashed potatoes

1 KG (2 LB 4 OZ) BABY NEW POTATOES (CHATS), UNPEELED
60 ML (¼ CUP) OLIVE OIL
SEA SALT

Preheat the oven to 180°C (350°F/Gas 4). Line a baking tray.

Boil the potatoes for 10–20 minutes, or until soft. Drain well and scatter the cooked potatoes on the prepared tray and, using a potato masher, squash the potatoes until flattened. Drizzle with the oil and generously sprinkle with the salt. Roast for 1 hour, or until dark golden and crisp.

Serves 8

This is one of our most popular lunch dishes at Café Arno. It is light, fresh and full of great flavours. The caramelised leeks work so well with the asparagus and salmon and a soft poached egg is a great addition.

Poached salmon salad with lemon dressing

4 x 200 G (7 oz) SALMON FILLETS,
    SKINNED AND PIN-BONED
500 ML (2 CUPS) WHITE WINE
500 ML (2 CUPS) WATER
2 FRESH BAY LEAVES
SEA SALT AND FRESHLY GROUND
    BLACK PEPPER
1 TABLESPOON OLIVE OIL
3 LEEKS, WHITE PART ONLY
100 G (½ CUP) SUGAR
1 BUNCH ASPARAGUS
4 LARGE HANDFULS MIXED
    LETTUCE AND BABY SPINACH
    LEAVES
1 RED ONION, FINELY SLICED
2 TOMATOES, EACH CUT INTO 6
2 TEASPOONS SALTED BABY
    CAPERS, WELL RINSED AND
    DRAINED, ROUGHLY CHOPPED

LEMON DRESSING

60 ML (¼ CUP) WHITE WINE
    VINEGAR
2 TEASPOONS DIJON MUSTARD
170 ML (⅔ CUP) OLIVE OIL
2 TEASPOONS SALTED BABY
    CAPERS, WELL RINSED AND
    DRAINED
125 G (4½ OZ/½ CUP) MAYONNAISE
3 TEASPOONS LEMON JUICE
1 TABLESPOON MAPLE SYRUP

To poach the salmon, put the wine, water, bay leaves, 1 teaspoon of salt and ½ teaspoon of pepper in a saucepan wide enough to fit the fish in one layer. Bring to the boil. Slip in the salmon fillets, cover with a lid and remove the pan from the heat. Poach the salmon for 10 minutes, or until cooked to your liking. Remove the fillets from the water, allow to cool to room temperature. Tear into large chunks to serve.

To make the caramelised leek, cut the leek into thickly sliced rounds, heat the olive oil in a frying pan over medium heat and gently fry the leek with the sugar and a pinch of salt. Stir until the leek is soft and golden, about 20 minutes. Set aside.

Lightly oil the asparagus and cook on a ridged grill pan or barbecue until slightly charred.

To make the dressing, blend the vinegar and mustard in a small food processor or blender. Slowly add the oil, continuing to blend. Add the capers and mayonnaise, one spoon at a time, followed by the lemon juice and maple syrup, blending after each addition. Season with salt and pepper.

Place the salad leaves, red onion, asparagus and tomato on a platter. Drizzle with a bit of the dressing and gently toss, trying to keep the vegetables on top of the leaves. Place the poached salmon on top, scatter with the caramelised leek and the capers, then drizzle on more dressing and gently mix again.

Serves 4

GLENDA REICHMAN

Sydney became home in 1990 when my husband, Barry, and I moved here as newlyweds from Benoni in South Africa.

My maternal grandmother passed away when my mother was young. In the short time they had together, she imparted her love of food as well as her wonderful recipes to my mother, who was then left with three brothers and her father to care for.

Imagine my mother's joy when she had two daughters of her own with whom she could then share these recipes. Sadly, I also lost my mother when she was quite young. My fondest memory of cooking with her was in preparation for her legendary second day lunch feast at Rosh Hashanah. She made sure that none of the 45 family and friends went hungry and that everyone's favourite dish was made. My sister and I spent many long hours by her side in the kitchen, helping and learning at the same time. This became an annual tradition of bonding and togetherness that I will never forget.

My mother loved nothing more than our family sharing mealtimes and special occasions together. I loved going into the kitchen, sitting on the countertop, watching her create these dishes and – my favourite – eating the little bit that she had saved for me.

I wanted my boys to love and appreciate the food of my heritage, but I have had no luck getting them to enjoy my mum's curried fish balls, gefilte fish, halva ice cream or ginger cake. Luckily I did hit the jackpot with pies. This recipe is a family favourite and a tribute to my mother, who would so love to be enjoying these pies with her grandsons.

Beef and potato pie

2 ONIONS, CHOPPED
60 ML (¼ CUP) OLIVE OIL
1.5 KG (3 LB 5 OZ) BLADE STEAK OR
    STEWING BEEF, CUBED
1 x 400 G (14 OZ) TIN DICED
    ITALIAN TOMATOES
125 ML (½ CUP) TOMATO SAUCE
    (KETCHUP)
60 ML (¼ CUP) BARBECUE SAUCE
1 TABLESPOON SOY SAUCE
1½ TEASPOONS DRIED ITALIAN
    HERBS
1½ TEASPOONS Season All
    SEASONED SALT (SEE NOTE)
½ TEASPOON SEA SALT
60 ML (¼ CUP) WATER
2 POTATOES, DICED
½ CUP (80 G/2¾ OZ) PEAS
4 SHEETS READY-MADE PUFF
    PASTRY

In a large frying pan or flameproof casserole dish, gently fry the onion in the oil until softened, about 10 minutes. Add the meat in batches and brown all over. Add the tomatoes, tomato sauce, barbecue sauce, soy sauce, dried herbs, Season All, salt and water. Stir and bring to the boil, then reduce the heat to low. Simmer, covered, for 1 hour, stirring from time to time.

Add the potato to the pan and simmer for another 30 minutes. Add the peas and simmer for a final 30 minutes, stirring from time to time. Remove the lid for the last 30 minutes if there is too much liquid in the dish. You want a little liquid left in the bottom but not too much. It will dry out a little more when baked under the pastry. Cool slightly before using.

Preheat the oven to 200°C (400°F/Gas 6). You will need a 2.5–3 litre (10–12 cup) pie or casserole dish.

To assemble the pie, if you want pastry on the bottom as well as the top, roll out and line the bottom and sides of the dish with pastry (optional). Fill the dish with the cooled meat mixture. Cover the top with a layer of pastry and trim to fit. Seal around the edge by pushing down with a fork. Make a few slits with a knife in the top of the pie. Bake for 45 minutes until golden and the pastry is cooked through. Remove from the oven and allow to stand for 15 minutes before serving.

Serves 6–8

NOTE: Season All contains chilli, black pepper, celery seeds, nutmeg, ground coriander, onion, paprika and garlic.

Photo on page 68

{Beef Bourguignon}

PAUL GORDON

Unhappy with the political situation in South Africa, my parents made the decision to move the family when I was just a young child. We made the long journey to Australia and settled in Adelaide, ready to start a new life. Not having any family around us, cooking became an important connection to my family's roots, Polish/Belarusian on one side and Lithuanian on the other.

I learned to cook at my mother's knee, observing as she made kneidlach at Pesach, or almond tarts on special occasions. I have vivid memories of waking up late in the night and seeing my mother and grandmother, who was visiting at the time, rolling the dough for teiglach *(South African biscuits soaked in syrup). If I was lucky, I was allowed to help cut the dough and watch as they dipped it into the rich syrup.*

Since then, my love of cooking has grown. Food and cooking now form an important part of my relationship with my wife, Jasmine. We've travelled the world together, trying new foods and learning new recipes. To me, sharing a dish provides a far better reminder of a place and people than a photograph ever could.

This recipe takes me back to the taste of France. It was taught to me by Caroline, the owner of a bed and breakfast we stayed in while travelling through Burgundy. I've subsequently made a few changes, but the core of the recipe stays the same. While the ingredients may seem simple, they work beautifully together. This dish is best served with a glass of French red and good friends.

Beef Bourguignon

4 TABLESPOONS PLAIN (ALL-PURPOSE) FLOUR (ENOUGH TO COAT THE BEEF)

1 TEASPOON SWEET PAPRIKA

1 TEASPOON SEA SALT

60 ML (¼ CUP) OLIVE OIL

1 KG (2 LB 4 OZ) GRAVY OR STEWING BEEF, CUBED

8 FRENCH SHALLOTS, PEELED AND HALVED, OR 1 LARGE ONION, FINELY CHOPPED

1 CUP (120 G/4 OZ) SMALL BUTTON MUSHROOMS

400 ML (1⅔ CUPS) RED WINE

400 ML (1⅔ CUPS) BEST-QUALITY BEEF STOCK

1 LARGE BOUQUET GARNI (SEE NOTE)

1 FRESH BAY LEAF

FRESHLY GROUND BLACK PEPPER

Mix the flour, paprika and salt in a large shallow dish, and toss the beef in it to coat.

Heat a little of the oil in a heavy-based flameproof casserole dish over medium heat and brown the beef, in batches, until golden brown. Set aside. Add more oil to the dish, and fry the shallots or onion until soft and translucent, stirring frequently, scraping up any caramelised bits from the bottom of the dish. Add the mushrooms and toss through.

Return the beef to the dish and add the wine, scraping the bottom of the dish again if needed. Bring to the boil for a minute, then add the stock, bouquet garni and bay leaf. If necessary, add more water or stock to barely cover the beef. Return to a simmer, cover and cook for 2½ hours, turning once or twice, until the meat is soft and fork tender. You can also cook it in the oven at 150°C (300°F/Gas 2) for the same length of time. Top up with water or stock if and when necessary, or if there is too much liquid, remove the lid for the last 15 minutes of cooking. Season to taste.

Serve with mashed potato or potato and onion gratin (see page 175).

Serves 4–6

NOTE: Bouquet garni is a bundle of herbs that usually includes thyme, parsley and bay leaves. It can be bought as an infusion bag in the spice section of food stores.

Photo on page 93

A Shabbat favourite with my sons and extended family, this recipe employs the usual Chinese ingredients, but delivers wonderfully rich-tasting sticky ribs. In keeping with my tradition of sharing recipes, the original came from my friend Aviva Teperman, but it can be tweaked to suit personal taste. Cook the ribs slowly with love and lots of basting. This recipe works equally well with beef top ribs or asado-style ribs (cut across the bone).

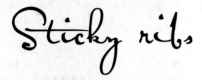

Sticky ribs

3 KG (6 LB 12 OZ) BEEF SHORT RIBS

SAUCE
250 ML (1 CUP) TOMATO SAUCE
  (KETCHUP)
250 ML (1 CUP) PLUM SAUCE
125 ML (½ CUP) HOISIN SAUCE
230 G (⅔ CUP) HONEY
1½ TABLESPOONS
  WORCESTERSHIRE SAUCE
3 CLOVES GARLIC, BRUISED

Preheat the oven to 180°C (350°F/Gas 4).

Combine all the sauce ingredients in a bowl.

Place the ribs in a roasting tin and cover with the sauce. Cover tightly with two layers of foil. Roast for 30 minutes, then reduce the temperature to 160°C (315°F/Gas 2–3) and cook for a further 3 hours, or until the ribs are fork tender. Remove the foil and cook for another 30–60 minutes until the ribs are brown and sticky. Check from time to time, turning once or twice and adding water to the bottom of the pan if it dries out.

Serves 6

As youngsters growing up in Melbourne, my brother and I were incredibly fussy eaters and would not eat anything green or red, and absolutely no cooked vegetables. Our Czech/Slovak parents' friends wondered why our mother didn't have a heart attack worrying about us! We had grown up, after all, surrounded by Eastern European delicacies.

As a teenager I started baking, and often cooked family meals if my mother was busy. Later I experienced the high-pressure, crazy environment of a kibbutz kitchen, then after my children were born, I have fond memories of my two-year-old son helping me prepare chocolate mousse for Seder from his highchair and sharing pakepakes (pancakes, as he called them) every Sunday morning. Fast forward 40 years, and now, as Friday night dinner approaches, my phone rings non-stop with extended family members making requests and offering suggestions. For me, cooking is a giving activity; I do it for relaxation, creativity, and enjoyment, and the simple pleasure I get from sharing with others.

My good friend Susie made this salad regularly for her family. Originally they loved it, but then ate it so often they made her promise not to make it anymore; she did not serve it again for many years. The joke is I call it Susie's beetroot salad but she hardly ever makes it.

Beetroot and herb salad

75 G (½ CUP) PISTACHIO NUTS,
    CHOPPED
2 LARGE BEETROOT (BEETS),
    PEELED
2 TABLESPOONS EXTRA VIRGIN
    OLIVE OIL
60 ML (¼ CUP) POMEGRANATE
    MOLASSES
2 TEASPOONS ROSEWATER
    (OPTIONAL)
JUICE OF 1 LEMON
1 BUNCH CHIVES, CHOPPED
½ BUNCH MINT, LEAVES CHOPPED
½ BUNCH FLAT-LEAF (ITALIAN)
    PARSLEY, LEAVES CHOPPED
½ BUNCH DILL, FRONDS CHOPPED
SEEDS FROM 1 POMEGRANATE

Toast the pistachio nuts for 5–10 minutes in a 160°C (315°F/Gas 2–3) oven or in a frying pan until lightly coloured and fragrant. Allow to cool.

Grate the beetroot into a bowl.

Make the dressing by mixing together the olive oil, pomegranate molasses, rosewater and lemon juice in a small bowl or jar, then pour over the beetroot and stir through.

Just before serving, toss through the chopped herbs, pistachio nuts and pomegranate seeds.

Serves 8–10

This delicious frozen lemon meringue is my all-time go-to gluten-free recipe, which I like to change sometimes by experimenting with different toppings and flavours. Once made, it is stored in the freezer and then taken out approximately 20 minutes before serving. The lemon syrup makes it a perfect decadent do-ahead dessert.

Frozen lemon meringue

MERINGUE DISCS

4 EGG WHITES

¼ TEASPOON CREAM OF TARTAR

2 TEASPOONS CORNFLOUR
    (CORNSTARCH)

225 G (8 OZ) CASTER (SUPERFINE)
    SUGAR

LEMON CUSTARD

4 EGG YOLKS

125 G (4½ OZ) CASTER (SUPERFINE)
    SUGAR

125 ML (½ CUP) LEMON JUICE

FINELY GRATED ZEST OF
    2 LEMONS

300 ML (1⅓ CUPS) THICKENED
    (WHIPPING) CREAM

LEMON SYRUP
(OPTIONAL)

FINELY GRATED ZEST OF ½ LEMON

60 ML (¼ CUP) LEMON JUICE,
    STRAINED

2 TABLESPOONS SUGAR

Start this recipe the day before serving.

Preheat the oven to 150°C (300°F/Gas 2). Line two baking trays with baking paper which have been marked with three 20 cm (8 inch) diameter circles or 28 x 12 cm (11 x 4¾ inch) rectangles.

To make the meringue discs, sprinkle the egg whites with the cream of tartar and whisk until stiff. Mix the cornflour with the sugar, then add to the egg whites, 1 tablespoon at a time, whisking well after each addition. Whisk for a few more minutes until thick and glossy. Using a spatula, spread the meringue inside the marked outlines, smoothing out to the edges. Place in the oven, reduce the temperature to 140°C (275°F/Gas 1) and bake for 1 hour, or until the meringue discs are crisp to touch and will lift off the paper easily. Place on a wire rack to cool completely.

Start making the lemon custard as soon as the meringues go in the oven, as it must be quite cold before the cream is folded in. Put the egg yolks and sugar in a heavy-based saucepan. Over a low heat, mix until smooth and well combined, then add the lemon juice and zest. Continue to stir constantly until the mixture thickens and coats the back of a spoon, about 10–15 minutes. Remove from the heat and stir for another minute. Pour into a bowl and refrigerate until completely cold, or place over a bowl of ice to cool faster. In a separate bowl, whip the cream until firm, then gently fold it into the cooled lemon custard one spoon at a time, until combined. Refrigerate until needed.

Set aside the best meringue disc to be the top. To assemble, place one meringue disc on a piece of baking paper and top it with half of the lemon custard. Do not spread the custard all the way to the edge; when you place the next disc on top, it will spread. Repeat with another layer of meringue and the remaining filling, then top with the final meringue layer. Wrap gently in foil then freeze for several hours or overnight. This can be done several days ahead.

To make the lemon syrup, combine all the syrup ingredients in a small saucepan, stirring over low heat until the sugar dissolves. Simmer, without stirring, for about 5 minutes, or until slightly thickened and tacky. Allow to cool to room temperature.

Remove the lemon meringue from the freezer 30 minutes before serving. Drizzle the lemon syrup over the top.

Serves 8–10

Photo on page 102

{Frozen lemon meringue}

{Cinnamon cake}

VARDA GOODMAN

I have a very close cousin in Los Angeles and on one of her visits we awoke to the delectable aroma of cinnamon. Margo had just whipped up this delicious cake, which has now become a staple in our home. The original recipe is made with Osem Pudding mix but you can substitute other brands.

Cinnamon cake

60 G (1¾ OZ) **BUTTER**

60 G (2¾ OZ/½ CUP) **BROWN SUGAR**

2 **TABLESPOONS GROUND CINNAMON**

4 **EGGS**

345 G (12 OZ/1½ CUPS) **CASTER (SUPERFINE) SUGAR**

185 ML (¾ CUP) **VEGETABLE OIL**

225 G (8 OZ/1½ CUPS) **SELF-RAISING FLOUR**

80 G (2¾ OZ) **VANILLA PUDDING MIX**

125 ML (½ CUP) **ORANGE JUICE**

¼ CUP ICING (CONFECTIONERS') **SUGAR, FOR DUSTING**

Preheat the oven to 180°C (350°F/Gas 4). Generously butter and flour a 2.5 litre (10 cup) non-stick bundt tin.

Melt the butter with the brown sugar and cinnamon. Set aside.

Whisk the eggs and caster sugar until light and fluffy. Beat in the oil, then add the flour, pudding mix and juice and mix until combined. Pour three quarters of the cake batter into the prepared tin and drizzle with the cinnamon mixture, then add the rest of the cake mixture.

Bang the tin once, then place in the oven and bake for 45 minutes, or until a skewer inserted comes out clean. Immediately turn the cake out onto a wire rack to cool, to avoid sticking. Dust with icing sugar to serve.

Serves 10–12

Photo on page 103

Our kitchen has never been a woman's domain. My father smokes his own chickens, whips up amazing scones on a Sunday morning and can produce not only a great curry but a great wine. The whole family is included in his winemaking enterprise, which has now become a beloved annual tradition and produces our sweet Shabbat and Pesach drop. Because of Dad, the men in my family are all at ease at the stove or with a recipe book, and I am so happy the skill and enthusiasm has passed on to my sons.

Originally from Johannesburg, when I was young we lived in Israel for seven years, then returned to South Africa until after I married. I grew up eating my mother's legendary Sunday roasts alongside traditional Jewish food, enriched by delicious Israeli cuisine.

We always knew South Africa would not be our home, and my husband and I happily arrived in Sydney in the early 1990s. Growing up in a home where food and family went hand-in-hand, it really doesn't matter where our extended family has landed. As soon as we are around a table, it is just like old times.

My granddad insisted that Grandma have a tin of wholemeal biscuits made at all times, as he didn't eat a lot of the richer treats she used to make. He thought they were healthy. No one had the heart to tell him they were full of sugar and butter. This recipe is a more modern version that I make for morning tea snacks in lunchboxes.

Fancy wholemeal biscuits

200 G (7 OZ) BUTTER, AT ROOM
   TEMPERATURE
220 G (7¾ OZ/1 CUP FIRMLY PACKED)
   BROWN SUGAR
2 TABLESPOONS GOLDEN SYRUP
   (LIGHT TREACLE)
1 EGG
150 G (5½ OZ/1 CUP) WHOLEMEAL
   (WHOLE-WHEAT) FLOUR
1 TEASPOON BAKING POWDER
75 G (2¾ OZ/½ CUP) PLAIN (ALL-
   PURPOSE) FLOUR
90 G (1 CUP) DESICCATED
   COCONUT
50 G (½ CUP) ROLLED (PORRIDGE) OATS
70 G (1 CUP) ALL-BRAN (BREAKFAST
   CEREAL) OR OTHER WHEAT-BRAN
   CEREAL
120 G (¾ CUP) SUNFLOWER SEEDS

Preheat the oven to 180°C (350°F/Gas 4). You will need two lined baking trays.

In an electric mixer, cream together the butter, sugar and golden syrup. Add the egg and mix well. If you prefer a more rustic biscuit, simply fold through the remaining ingredients by hand. Otherwise, add the remaining ingredients to the electric mixer and and once they have combined to form a rough dough, beat for a minute or two longer to break down the ingredients a little more. Form into a ball, cover with plastic wrap and refrigerate for 15 minutes.

Roll out the dough between two sheets of well-floured baking paper to a thickness of 3–5 mm (⅛–¼ inch). Cut into squares with a floured knife or cut out rounds with a 5.5 cm (2¼ inch) floured cookie cutter and place on the prepared trays. Bake for 12–15 minutes or until golden.

Makes approximately 80 biscuits
Store in an airtight container

I grew up baking. My grandmother was a renowned baker in New Zealand and my sister and I used to sit in her kitchen watching her cook. All the fruits and vegetables she used were from my grandfather's organic biodynamic garden where we loved to help pick ingredients before we started cooking.

In Johannesburg my husband, Mark, and I ran a corporate catering business for five years, and we had our own Japanese restaurant for a short time.

In 1994 we made the move to Adelaide with our three baby daughters, and soon welcomed a son. My background of making fresh preserves, jams, pickles and condiments from my childhood stays with me, but I love yeast bakery the most. Challahs, babkes and bulkas are churned out for Shabbat in our household, and my pane acido, sourdough starter, is coming up for its tenth birthday, although it takes a vacation in the freezer over Pesach. (See also Justine's Sufganiot recipe in Tradition, page 286.)

This is my sister Jo's recipe. Jo has many skills and interests but cooking is not top of the list; however, she maintains you only have to know how to make a few things well and this chocolate cake certainly fits the bill. She makes this cake for every birthday, whether family or friend. It is a great cake for the kids to take to school – my boys literally queue up for a piece when she brings one over. They love my sister but I think they love her cake more! – Paula Horwitz

Glazed chocolate birthday cake

300 G (10½ OZ/2 CUPS) PLAIN
  (ALL-PURPOSE) FLOUR
460 G (1 LB ¼ OZ/2 CUPS) CASTER
  (SUPERFINE) SUGAR
250 ML (1 CUP) WATER
25 G (1 OZ/¼ CUP) BEST-QUALITY
  COCOA POWDER
60 ML (¼ CUP) VEGETABLE OIL
120 G (4¼ OZ) BUTTER
2 EGGS, LIGHTLY WHISKED
125 ML (½ CUP) BUTTERMILK
1 TEASPOON VANILLA EXTRACT
1 TEASPOON BICARBONATE OF
  SODA (BAKING SODA)

ICING
60 G (2¼ OZ) BUTTER
2 TABLESPOONS BUTTERMILK
2 TABLESPOONS BEST-QUALITY
  COCOA POWDER
160 G (1 CUP) ICING
  (CONFECTIONERS') SUGAR

Preheat the oven to 180°C (350°F/Gas 4). Grease and line a rectangular baking tin, approximately 32 x 22 x 4 cm (12¾ x 8½ x 1½ inches).

In a large bowl, combine the flour and sugar with a wooden spoon.

In a small saucepan, combine the water, cocoa, oil and butter. Heat until combined and the butter is melted.

Add the warm mixture to the dry ingredients and stir until combined.

In a separate bowl, mix together the eggs, buttermilk, vanilla and bicarbonate of soda. Add to the flour and butter mixture in the large bowl and mix until well combined. Pour into the prepared tin and bake for 20–30 minutes, or until cooked through and a skewer inserted in the middle comes out clean.

While the cake is in the oven, prepare the icing by melting the butter and mixing with the buttermilk and cocoa. Stir well to combine. Add the icing sugar, mixing well until the icing is smooth.

As soon as the cake is removed from the oven, pour the icing over the top.

Serves 16

Read Paula's story on page 16

Comfort

Food that feels like home. I'm drawn to the recipes that warm our hearts and soothe our souls. I love slow cooking for cold nights, dishes that make my children smile, soups to nourish and sustain friends in need, puddings reminiscent of childhood. There's nothing better for me than spending an afternoon kneading and baking chocolate cugloaf, the comforting aromas filling our home, bringing with it the memories of generations gone by.

Natanya ♡

Recipes

{Prune and chocolate cake}

My mother would come home from the markets with great excitement if she found fresh borlotti beans. That night we would have her prized Turkish baked beans – made with only the freshest beans – as part of mezze, an array of many beautifully made dishes.

Turkish baked beans

500 G (1 LB 2 OZ) FRESH BORLOTTI
    BEANS (UNSHELLED)
½ ONION, FINELY CHOPPED
2 CARROTS, FINELY CHOPPED
1 TABLESPOON OLIVE OIL, PLUS
    EXTRA, FOR SERVING
140 G (5 OZ) TOMATO PASTE
    (CONCENTRATED PURÉE)
250 ML (1 CUP) WATER
½ TEASPOON SWEET PAPRIKA
1 TEASPOON SEA SALT
FRESHLY GROUND BLACK PEPPER

Shell the beans, then boil in water until just tender, about 20 minutes. Drain and set aside.

In a saucepan over medium heat, sauté the onion and carrot in the oil until softened. Add the tomato paste, water and beans. Cook for about 30 minutes, or until thick and the beans are fully cooked. Add a little more olive oil and season with the paprika, salt and pepper.

Serves 6 as a side dish

I was only five years old when we emigrated from Turkey. My beautiful mother, Sevin, as a young bride, worked very hard to make a new life in Australia, and it was always important to put a cooked meal on the table for my father, a man of tradition.

Growing up, there was always something soaking; maybe lentils, chickpeas or beans. This inspired my love of cooking legumes and using them in many traditional Turkish dishes.

As the main cook in our family, I am also always soaking, pickling and experimenting, and finding the flavours and smells that were part of my childhood home. We have two children; our daughter is a vegetarian and our son a meat lover. Talia loves beans because they are essential for her health, while for Tyssen they are essential for taste.

My regular trips to Turkey with my wife, Robyn, continue to fuel my love of Turkish cuisine. The key is fresh and simple but the staple ingredient I learned from my mother is love.

My mother passed away a few years ago at a young 62 years. Cooking her recipes has been a way to heal my loss, and these dishes keep her memory very much alive. (See also Ata's clay pot snapper with burghul pilaf on page 80.)

ATA GOKYILDIRIM

My mother's yoghurt soup was one of her favourites. She prepared it using her own creamy, slightly sour, homemade yoghurt, creating a warm, comforting and very special winter's soup.

Yoghurt soup

1 EGG
750 G (1 LB 10 OZ/3 CUPS) GREEK-
　STYLE YOGHURT
75 G (⅓ CUP) FRENCH-STYLE GREEN
　LENTILS
750 ML (3 CUPS) RICH VEGETABLE
　STOCK
110 G (½ CUP) BASMATI RICE
SEA SALT AND FRESHLY GROUND
　BLACK PEPPER
DRIED MINT, FOR SERVING

Beat the egg into the yoghurt and set aside.

Bring a saucepan of water to the boil and add the lentils. Boil until cooked, about 20 minutes, then drain.

In a separate saucepan, bring the stock to the boil and add the rice. Turn the heat to low and cook for about 15 minutes, or until the rice is very soft but there is still stock in the pan. Remove the pan from the heat, add the yoghurt mixture, then the lentils. Stir well and season to taste, adding more stock if it is too thick. Sprinkle with the dried mint to serve.

Serve warm in small bowls.

Serves 12

NOTE: The stock for this soup needs to be very flavoursome. For a rich stock, bring 1 litre (4 cups) vegetable stock to a boil and reduce to 750 ml (3 cups).

Photo on page 113

This simple and comforting dish is considered easy to digest – with little spice and no meat – so we like to take it to friends when they feel unwell. My children find this a particularly nurturing dish and it has become one of their favourites.

Spinach healing rice

1½ BUNCHES ENGLISH SPINACH
OR SILVERBEET (SWISS CHARD)
2 TABLESPOONS OLIVE OIL
½ ONION, FINELY CHOPPED
220 G (1 CUP) BASMATI RICE,
WASHED AND DRAINED
625 ML (2½ CUPS) CHICKEN OR
VEGETABLE STOCK
SEA SALT AND FRESHLY GROUND
BLACK PEPPER
PLAIN YOGHURT, FOR SERVING
(OPTIONAL)

Remove and discard the stems from the spinach or silverbeet and roughly chop the leaves.

Choose a deep frying pan with a firm-fitting lid. Heat the oil over medium heat and fry the onion for 10 minutes, or until soft. Add the spinach or silverbeet, rice and stock, and stir. Season with salt and pepper. Bring to the boil, cover, then reduce the heat to very low and cook for 12 minutes until the rice is cooked.

Serve with the yoghurt, if desired.

Serves 6 as a side dish

Photo on page 113

This simple, warming and unique recipe comes from Savta Malka. Each and every time we enjoy this soup at home, the tale continues to be retold around the family table with the warmest memories of our beloved.

Lubiya—Sephardi soup

185 G (1 CUP) DRIED BLACK-EYED
   PEAS
2 ONIONS, FINELY CHOPPED
2 CLOVES GARLIC, CRUSHED
1 TABLESPOON OLIVE OIL
1 TEASPOON GROUND CUMIN
1 TEASPOON GROUND TURMERIC
1 BIRD'S EYE CHILLI, FINELY
   CHOPPED
½ TEASPOON SALT
1 X 400 G (14 OZ) TIN DICED
   ITALIAN TOMATOES
625 ML (2½ CUPS) CHICKEN OR
   VEGETABLE STOCK
SEA SALT AND FRESHLY GROUND
   BLACK PEPPER

Start this recipe the day before serving.

Place the black-eyed peas in a bowl and cover with plenty of water. Set aside and soak overnight. Drain the peas, rinse under cold water and drain again.

In a large saucepan over low to medium heat, fry the onion and garlic in the oil for 15 minutes, or until soft. Add the cumin, turmeric and chilli and cook for 2–3 minutes, or until fragrant. Add all the other ingredients and cook for 1 hour, or until the peas are soft, adding more water if the soup becomes too thick. Season to taste with salt and pepper and serve with crusty bread.

Serves 4

I am a Sabra – born and bred in Israel – from Kibbutz Zikim on the Mediterranean coast. My wife, Johanne, and I married in Israel and had our first daughter, Leah. When she was eighteen months old we moved to Goondiwindi in outback Queensland for my irrigation business. We now have a family of three children.

We often marvel at our grandmother Savta Malka's love of soup and the story of why she would always eat it after her main meal and not as a starter as most people would.

Savta's parents left Russia in the early 1900s. They explained to her that the Jewish people were living in difficult times and were never sure when they would next be uprooted from their homes. At mealtimes, they would fill their bellies first with the main course and eat the soup afterwards. If they had to hurriedly depart their homes due to pogroms or persecution, they would at least have a solid meal on which to survive. So she has always made us think it's best to leave your soup till last.

TRACEY ISACOWITZ AND KERRY RABIE

SISTERS

Our family came to Australia from South Africa over 30 years ago. Our mum, Maureen Flekser, lost her dad when she was only four and was taken in by our grandmother Rose, so she lived in a house with her sister, aunts and grandmother. With that many women under one roof, cooking was bound to be an important aspect of their lives.

Mum is a wonderful cook, and growing up we spent many happy times in her kitchen, along with our sister, Lori. There wasn't a Pesach or Rosh Hashanah where we didn't gather together to make bulkas, kichel, kneidlach, geschmirte matzo and other favourites. Our mum was the dessert queen. She would often make metre-high croquembouches with a web of spun sugar for special occasions, and our birthday cakes were decorated elaborately. Our dad, Hymie, having the world's sweetest tooth, was always waiting in the background to lick the bowl – raw or cooked!

Years later, the kitchen is now the heart and soul of both our homes. Food for us is a journey of experimenting, tasting and trialling, with much discussion, criticism and praise. It is time spent together. With thanks to Mum and our ancestors we now pass this passion onto our children.

Kerry loves any opportunity to gather ideas from magazines in a doctor's or dentist's waiting room, remembering the basic ingredients and then manipulating them – which is how this soup evolved. It started off as Kerry's mushroom and barley soup, but was then passed on to some of Tracey's friends, who then named it Tracey's mushroom and barley soup. It is now Kerry and Tracey's mushroom and barley soup! Either way, it's delicious and hearty.

Mushroom and barley soup

10 G (¼ OZ) DRIED PORCINI
   MUSHROOMS
250 ML (1 CUP) BOILING WATER
1 TABLESPOON OLIVE OIL
1 LARGE ONION, CHOPPED
1 CELERY STALK, CHOPPED
1 LARGE CARROT, CHOPPED
500 G (1 LB 2 OZ) MUSHROOMS,
   SLICED
1 LITRE (4 CUPS) VEGETABLE STOCK
150 G (⅔ CUP) PEARL BARLEY,
   RINSED
SEA SALT AND FRESHLY GROUND
   BLACK PEPPER
1 HANDFUL CHOPPED FLAT-LEAF
   (ITALIAN) PARSLEY

Soak the porcini mushrooms in the boiling water for 15 minutes.

Heat the oil in a large saucepan over medium heat and add the onion, celery and carrot. Fry until soft, about 10 minutes. Stir in the sliced mushrooms and cook until soft, about 10 minutes.

Strain the porcini mushrooms, reserving the liquid.

Add the stock, porcini mushrooms and the reserved liquid to the pan. Then add the barley and bring to the boil. Reduce the heat to low and simmer for 1 hour, adding extra water if the soup becomes too thick. Season well with salt and pepper. Stir through the parsley before serving.

Serves 6–8

This is a dish that my aunty, Myrna Abadee, used to make often, as she would always have it ready in the fridge when friends dropped in for a bite. It is home cooking at its most heartwarming. I imagine the addition of tomato soup was introduced in Australia, when she tried to replicate the flavours of her own childhood. The flavours do improve if allowed to sit in the fridge for a couple of days. – Lisa Goldberg

Aunty Myrna's cabbage rolls

1 GREEN CABBAGE

SAUCE

2 ONIONS, CHOPPED

60 ML (¼ CUP) VEGETABLE OIL

1 x 420 G (14¾ OZ) TIN CONDENSED
   TOMATO SOUP

400 ML TOMATO PASSATA (PURÉED
   TOMATOES)

1 x 400 G (14 OZ) TIN DICED
   ITALIAN TOMATOES

JUICE OF 2 LEMONS

1½ TABLESPOONS SUGAR

1 TEASPOON SALT

½ TEASPOON FRESHLY GROUND
   BLACK PEPPER

FILLING

600 G (1 LB 5 OZ) MINCED (GROUND)
   TOPSIDE BEEF

2–3 CLOVES GARLIC

2 TEASPOONS SEA SALT

185 G (1 CUP) COOKED LONG-
   GRAIN RICE, ABOUT 100 G
   (½ CUP) UNCOOKED

1 ONION, GRATED

½ TEASPOON FRESHLY GROUND
   BLACK PEPPER

2 EGGS, LIGHTLY BEATEN

Start this recipe at least one day before serving, as the flavours develop overnight.

Core the cabbage and place in a large saucepan of cold water so that the cabbage is fully submerged. Bring to the boil and simmer for 15 minutes. Remove from the stovetop and allow to cool in the water. Strain when cool, separate the leaves and cut out the thick stalks with a knife.

To make the sauce, you will need a large saucepan. Fry the onion in the oil over low heat until soft, about 20 minutes. Add the remaining ingredients and simmer for 15 minutes. Taste for seasoning. Set aside until needed.

To make the filling, put the beef in a medium-sized bowl. On a chopping board, using the back of a knife, press the garlic with the salt to form a paste. Add to the beef, along with the rice, onion and pepper. Season generously. Add the eggs and combine.

To make the parcels, lay ¼ cup of the filling in an oblong shape in the centre of a cabbage leaf. Fold in the ends and then roll up like a parcel. Place in the sauce, seam side down. Continue with all the filling and cabbage leaves, placing the rolls snugly side by side in the sauce. Any unused or torn leaves can be rolled up and stuffed into the gaps in the pan. Make sure all the rolls are covered with sauce. Bring to a simmer, cover and cook for 3 hours, basting from time to time. If the cabbage rolls start to dry out, add more water to cover.

Place in the refrigerator when cool and reheat to serve the next day.

Serves 8

Read Lisa's story on page 13

{Slow-cooked beef with ras el hanout}

This is a perfect meal for when it is cold outside. Growing up we often had similar slow-cooked aromatic dishes for Shabbat lunch. This recipe reminds me of my Savta Eto coming to our place in the afternoon to help my mother, making her spice mix and grating the tomatoes. The dish would sit on the platta *all night and the smell in the house on Shabbat morning was so warm and wonderful, making us feel happy to be home.*

Slow-cooked beef with ras el hanout

1 KG (2 LB 4 OZ) GRAVY OR STEWING
  BEEF, TRIMMED AND CUT INTO
  2.5 CM (1 INCH) PIECES
2 SMALL ONIONS, FINELY
  CHOPPED
2 CLOVES GARLIC, CRUSHED
2 TABLESPOONS OLIVE OIL
2 TEASPOONS RAS EL HANOUT
  SPICE MIX (SEE FOLLOWING
  RECIPE)
2 BIRD'S EYE CHILLIES, FINELY
  CHOPPED AND DESEEDED
¼ TEASPOON EACH SEA SALT
  AND FRESHLY GROUND BLACK
  PEPPER
4 TOMATOES
1½ PRESERVED LEMON QUARTERS
2 TEASPOONS HONEY
1 BUNCH CORIANDER (CILANTRO),
  ROUGHLY CHOPPED
1 BUNCH FLAT-LEAF (ITALIAN)
  PARSLEY, ROUGHLY CHOPPED

Preheat the oven to 140°C (275°F/Gas 1).

Place the beef in a deep casserole dish. Add the onion, garlic, oil, ras el hanout, chilli, salt and pepper and toss to combine.

Halve the tomatoes crossways, squeeze out and discard the seeds. Coarsely grate the tomatoes down to the skin, straight into the casserole. Discard the skins. Rinse the preserved lemon, remove the pulp and membrane and finely chop the rind. Add to the meat, reserving some for garnish. Add the honey and a small handful each of the coriander and parsley.

Stir well, cover and cook in the oven for at least 3½ hours, or until the meat is fork tender. The juices from the meat should keep the dish moist, but check after 1½ hours of cooking and add a little water if necessary.

When the meat is very tender, transfer to a serving dish, scatter over the preserved lemon rind and the remaining herbs.

Serves 4–6

Photo on page 123

RAS EL HANOUT

½ TEASPOON GROUND CLOVES

½ TEASPOON CAYENNE PEPPER

2 TEASPOONS GROUND ALLSPICE

2 TEASPOONS GROUND CUMIN

2 TEASPOONS GROUND GINGER

2 TEASPOONS GROUND TURMERIC

2 TEASPOONS FRESHLY GROUND
   BLACK PEPPER

2 TEASPOONS GROUND
   CARDAMOM

3 TEASPOONS GROUND
   CINNAMON

3 TEASPOONS GROUND
   CORIANDER

1½ TABLESPOONS FRESHLY
   GRATED NUTMEG

Combine all the spices in a jar, seal, shake well and store in a cool dark place.

Makes 60 g (2¼ oz)

MIRI COLLIS

I was born in Israel to a Moroccan family, the youngest of seven children. I remember coming home from school at the end of the week to find my parents in the kitchen preparing for Shabbat. Dad would take the freshly baked bread out of the oven and, while it was still warm, make me a sandwich of tomato dip, just-fried eggplant and a little morsel of the delicious meat we would all be eating later.

Having eaten what I still consider to be the best sandwich in the world, I would go straight into the kitchen and help with the preparations for our Friday night feast. When my dad and brothers came back from synagogue, the house would smell of Shabbat: warm and welcoming. The table would be set with many dips and salads, special wine and challah, and the rest of the dishes would be finished and ready to be served.

Now I have my own catering business, which I enjoy greatly. I am excited that food – something I am so passionate about – is such a major part of my life.

In my family, shakshouka was a meal we had when there was nothing in the house to eat, normally on a Sunday, the day after Shabbat. My parents knew how to cook the eggs on top perfectly, not too hard and not too soft. We used to simply scoop it up with bread and this is the way I still do it today. I think it is the only way to eat shakshouka!

Shakshouka eggs

2 KG (4 LB 8 OZ/ABOUT 20) ROMA
  (PLUM) TOMATOES
60 ML (¼ CUP) OLIVE OIL
2 LARGE (500 G/1 LB 2 OZ) GREEN
  CAPSICUMS (PEPPERS)
2 LONG GREEN CHILLIES
3 CLOVES GARLIC, CRUSHED
1 TEASPOON SEA SALT
¾ TEASPOON FRESHLY GROUND
  BLACK PEPPER
½ TEASPOON SWEET PAPRIKA
4–6 EGGS

Peel the tomatoes by cutting a small cross at the pointy end. Put the tomatoes in a large bowl and pour on boiling water to cover. After 10–15 minutes, peel the skin off and discard. Chop the tomatoes and place in a large saucepan. Add the oil and simmer over low to medium heat for 1½ hours, stirring often.

Preheat the oven to 220°C (425°F/Gas 7). Line a large baking tray. While the tomatoes are cooking, place the capsicums and chillies on the prepared tray and roast until slightly blackened and soft. The chillies will take about 10 minutes and the capsicums about 30 minutes. Remove from the oven, cover with foil to steam, and when cool enough to touch, peel, deseed and cut into strips.

Add the capsicum, chilli, garlic and spices to the tomatoes. Simmer, stirring regularly, for at least 1 hour, until thick, adding water if necessary. It is ready when the colour deepens and the flavour is rich. Taste for seasoning and add more if needed. The sauce can now be used immediately or stored in the fridge for several days, until you are ready to cook the eggs and serve.

To cook the eggs, reheat the shakshouka in a frying pan. Make 4–6 indentations where you wish the eggs to go. Gently crack the eggs into the indentations, turn the heat to low and cover with a lid. Poach the eggs for 5–15 minutes, or until cooked to your liking. Serve immediately.

Serves 4–6

When I make this dish, the whole house has an amazing aroma from the slow cooking. It is our family's winter favourite and they always insist I make extra so they can have it again the next night!

Osso buco with lentils

2 TABLESPOONS OLIVE OIL

1 KG (2 LB 4 OZ) VEAL OSSO BUCO

1 ONION, FINELY CHOPPED

1 CARROT, FINELY CHOPPED

2 CELERY STALKS, FINELY
    CHOPPED

3 CLOVES GARLIC, CRUSHED

2 ROSEMARY SPRIGS

½ BUNCH THYME

2 FRESH BAY LEAVES

3 WHOLE CLOVES

250 ML (1 CUP) WHITE WINE

1 X 400 G (14 OZ) TIN DICED
    ITALIAN TOMATOES

500 ML (2 CUPS) CHICKEN OR VEAL
    STOCK

225 G (1 CUP) French-STYLE
    GREEN LENTILS

1 HANDFUL CHOPPED FLAT-LEAF
    (ITALIAN) PARSLEY

Preheat the oven to 180°C (350°F/Gas 4).

Heat the olive oil in a flameproof casserole dish and fry the osso buco pieces in batches until well browned. Remove from the dish. Add the onion, carrot, celery and garlic and fry over medium heat for 10 minutes or until soft, adding more oil if necessary. Stir in the herbs, bay leaves and cloves.

Add the wine to the dish, bring to the boil and reduce by half. Add the tomatoes and 1½ cups of the stock, stir, then put the osso buco pieces into the sauce and bring to the boil. Cover the dish with a lid or a double sheet of foil and cook in the oven for 1 hour.

Add the lentils and the remaining stock to the dish, if needed, to ensure they have a little liquid to cook in. Return to the oven, turning and basting from time to time, for another 30 minutes, or until the meat is soft and almost falling off the bone.

Serves 4

Read Robin's story on page 160

I made this many times before it tasted exactly the same as my mother's – the Kalocsai brand of Hungarian paprika was the missing secret ingredient. We serve it with knockerli *(tiny flour dumplings) or fettuccine.*

Veal goulash

3 WHITE ONIONS, CHOPPED

60 ML (¼ CUP) PEANUT OIL

1 TABLESPOON SWEET PAPRIKA

1 KG (2 LB 4 OZ) VEAL SHOULDER OR
SHIN, CUBED

½ GREEN CAPSICUM (PEPPER),
CHOPPED

1 TOMATO, PEELED AND CHOPPED

2 TEASPOONS SEA SALT, OR TO
TASTE

2 TEASPOONS PLAIN (ALL-PURPOSE)
FLOUR OR CORNFLOUR
(CORNSTARCH), TO THICKEN

80 ML (⅓ CUP) WATER

In a large frying pan over medium heat, fry the onion in the oil until lightly golden, about 10 minutes. Stir in the paprika and the veal and fry for a few minutes until the veal changes colour.

Add the capsicum, tomato and salt to the pan. Cover with a lid and simmer over low heat for 1½ hours, or until fork tender, adding a little water if needed to stop it sticking.

About 10 minutes before the veal is ready, mix the flour with the water and mix through the goulash.

Serves 4–6

My grandmother had barely enough time to teach her newly married daughter how to cook before my parents fled Communist Hungary in 1948. Once settled in Sydney, my parents longed for the cakes of the café houses of Budapest and my mother spent hours recreating them.

My family sat together for breakfast and dinner every day. Family meals meant so much to my father, who had left his family at fifteen, and then sadly lost his parents in the war. As the only girl in the family, I was Mum's helper in the kitchen. For many years I would start each day squeezing eighteen oranges for breakfast, and by the time I was fifteen, I had mastered quite a few simple meals and cakes. I married a South African who had never eaten Hungarian food. Now it is our own family's comfort food, especially in the winter months, and I rarely entertain without one of my mum's cakes on the menu.

There are many versions of this dish, most of which involve a spicy Hungarian sausage. This is the version we grew up with. It is always great as part of a buffet, or on its own as a light meal with a salad. It is a favourite at Passover time, when we substitute matzo meal for the breadcrumbs.

Rakott krumpli

2 KG (4 LB 8 OZ) POTATOES, UNPEELED AND WASHED

8 EGGS

SEA SALT

100 G (3½ OZ) BUTTER

300 G (10½ OZ) SOUR CREAM

60 G (HEAPED ½ CUP) GRATED TASTY CHEESE

35 G (¼ CUP) DRY BREADCRUMBS

You will need to start this recipe the day before serving.

Boil the potatoes in salted water until cooked but still firm, about 10–15 minutes. Drain and leave in the pan with the lid on for 15 minutes. When cool, peel, cover with plastic wrap and refrigerate for several hours or overnight.

Boil the eggs until hard, about 8 minutes. Peel the eggs and refrigerate until needed.

Preheat the oven to 170°C (325°F/Gas 3). Grease a large 3 litre (12 cup) ovenproof dish.

To assemble the rakott krumpli, cut the potatoes into 5 mm (¼ inch) thick slices. Layer half the potatoes, overlapping with each other, into the bottom of the dish. Salt the potatoes. Slice all the eggs thinly with an egg slicer, and layer over the potatoes. Salt the eggs.

Melt the butter, add the sour cream and stir to combine over the heat until liquid.

Pour half the butter mixture over the potato and egg in the dish. Layer the remaining potatoes, salt and pour on the rest of the sour cream mixture. Scatter the cheese over the top and then sprinkle on the breadcrumbs or matzo meal. Cover with foil and bake for 20 minutes. Remove the foil and bake for a further 20–30 minutes, or until the top is golden and crisp.

Serves 8

This never fails to impress – it has a delicious flavour and a smell that fills the home. I always have a jar of morello cherries in the pantry, and within 45 minutes there can be a freshly baked sour cherry slice. It is perfect for afternoon tea.

Klarika's sour cherry slice

250 G (9 oz/1⅔ cups) **SELF-RAISING FLOUR**

250 G (9 oz/1 cup plus 1 tablespoon) **CASTER** (superfine) **SUGAR**

300 G (10½ oz) **SOUR CREAM**

2 EGG YOLKS

FINELY GRATED ZEST OF 1 LEMON

275 G (9¾ oz) **DRAINED PITTED MORELLO CHERRIES**

ICING (confectioners') **SUGAR, SIFTED, FOR DUSTING**

Preheat the oven to 170°C (325°F/Gas 3). Grease and line a 28 x 18 cm (11 x 7 inch) rectangular baking tin.

Put the flour, caster sugar, sour cream, egg yolks and lemon zest in a bowl and mix together with a fork. You can also do this in the food processor. Spoon the mixture into the prepared tin. The mixture is quite thick and hard to spread.

Place the cherries over the mixture, pushing them in a little. Bake for 35 minutes, or until cooked and golden.

Allow the slice to cool in the tin. When cool, cut into squares and dust with the icing sugar.

Makes 20–24 pieces

This compote was served as part of a very fine breakfast at the fabulous country-style B&B 'La Veduta', at Russell in the Bay of Islands, New Zealand. The lovely hosts, Danielle and Dino, graciously agreed to share the recipe with me – and now with other lovers of good food for this book. I have served it many times and friends always comment on how delicious it is. I associate the compote with long, unhurried breakfasts, relaxing with good friends and family.

Middle Eastern kompot

225 G (1 CUP) PITTED PRUNES,
 HALVED

225 G (1½ CUPS) DRIED APRICOTS,
 HALVED

100 G (½ CUP) SOFT DRIED FIGS,
 QUARTERED

100 G (⅔ CUP) RAISINS

100 G (⅔ CUP) BLANCHED ALMONDS

50 G (⅓ CUP) PINE NUTS

1 TEASPOON GROUND CINNAMON

¼ TEASPOON FRESHLY GRATED
 NUTMEG

50 G (¼ CUP) BROWN SUGAR

1 TABLESPOON ROSEWATER

ZEST AND JUICE OF 1 ORANGE

Start this recipe at least 1–2 days before serving.

Place all the ingredients in a large bowl and cover with cold water. Stir well and set aside in a cool place or the refrigerator for 1–2 days. Stir the compote a couple of times each day. Add more orange juice if the compote becomes too dry, it should be quite syrupy. Before serving, add more cinnamon and nutmeg to taste.

Serve with Greek-style yoghurt.

Makes 6 cups

I came to Australia from England in 1949, almost the same time my husband, John, arrived from Prague. My mother was an accomplished cook, yet my interest in cooking only came to me in my early twenties.

I was an inaugural member of WIZO Ilana in Adelaide, founded by my wonderful late mother-in-law, Roszi. The diverse group of young members opened my eyes to a vast and exciting array of dishes and recipes. It was a steep learning curve. When asked to bake meringues for a fundraiser, mine resembled coins compared to the fluffy tennis ball-sized ones from my more experienced peers. My poor husband suffered too in the early days, and I'm sure he loved going home to his mother's delicious Hungarian goulash with dumplings.

Needless to say, my culinary skills have dramatically improved thanks to 45 years of marriage, six years in Hong Kong, involvement in Adelaide's Jewish community, and living in multicultural South Australia. I love sharing recipes with my children and their spouses, and when my grandchildren join in as well, that's just the icing on the cake!

I first ate this at a friend's dinner party years ago, and just loved it. She kindly gave me her recipe, which I have adapted to my own taste. I like to use blood orange marmalade if it is available as it gives the dish a beautiful reddish hue. Just like the food my mother used to make, it is classic comfort food, with a stylish twist.

Orange bread and butter pudding

600 G (1 LB 5 OZ) BRIOCHE OR
  CHALLAH, CRUSTS REMOVED
  (NET WEIGHT 400 G)
150 G (5½ OZ) BUTTER, MELTED
3 ORANGES, PEELED AND
  SEGMENTED
225 G (½ CUP) BEST-QUALITY
  ORANGE MARMALADE
3 EGGS
500 ML (2 CUPS) PURE CREAM
  (35% FAT)
115 G (½ CUP) CASTER (SUPERFINE)
  SUGAR
FINELY GRATED ZEST OF 2
  ORANGES
3 TABLESPOONS DEMERARA OR
  RAW SUGAR

Preheat the oven to 180°C (350°F/Gas 4). Butter a 2.5 litre (10 cup) ovenproof dish, approximately 36 x 18 cm (14¼ x 7 inches).

Cut the brioche or challah into large rough chunks and place in the prepared dish. Pour the melted butter on top. Add the orange segments, tucking them in gently.

In a small saucepan, heat the marmalade over low heat until warm, then pour over the bread.

Beat together the eggs, cream and caster sugar. Mix in the orange zest and pour evenly over the bread mixture.

Sprinkle with the demerara or raw sugar and bake for 45 minutes to 1 hour, or until golden.

Serves 8–10

Growing up, Fridays were baking days. Of course my brothers and I were eager participants, our faces covered in chocolate and cake mixture as we 'helped' our mother whip up an array of hot milk sponges, chocolate cakes and enormous marble cakes.

I grew up in Wellington, a small country town outside Cape Town, surrounded by a family that loved food. I learned to cook from my grandmothers and my mother, who remains (at 80) an amazingly talented and innovative cook. My parents were generous and hospitable entertainers. My mother would twist traditions and was quite the trendsetter; I remember her matzo balls stuffed with chopped almonds and cinnamon and baked in the oven.

We immigrated to Australia in 1979. Although I live in Adelaide, my three children and grandson live in Melbourne, yet we still compare recipes and restaurants. In our family if we are not eating or preparing delicious food, we are talking about it.

Melktert or milk tart is a very popular dessert with a distinctive Dutch flavour, originating from the Afrikaans community in South Africa. There are of course many recipes available but our family and friends have voted my mum's the all-time best. She makes it whenever she has friends over for tea and has also been known to whip up ten or twenty for charity cake sales. They were always the first items to sell out. – Paula Horwitz

Melktert

PASTRY

150 G (5½ OZ/1 CUP) PLAIN (ALL-
  PURPOSE) FLOUR
100 G (3½ OZ) BUTTER, AT ROOM
  TEMPERATURE
2 TEASPOONS CASTER (SUPERFINE)
  SUGAR
PINCH OF SALT

FILLING

1 EGG
115 G (4 OZ/½ CUP) CASTER
  (SUPERFINE) SUGAR
1 TABLESPOON PLAIN (ALL-PURPOSE)
  FLOUR
1¼ TABLESPOONS CORNFLOUR
  (CORNSTARCH)
500 ML (2 CUPS) MILK
20 G (¾ OZ) BUTTER, ROUGHLY
  CHOPPED
1 TEASPOON VANILLA EXTRACT
GROUND CINNAMON, FOR
  DUSTING

Preheat the oven to 180°C (350°F/Gas 4). Grease a 24 cm (9½ inch) pie dish.

Place all the pastry ingredients in a food processor and process quickly until a ball of soft dough is just formed. Alternatively, combine by hand in a bowl.

Press the dough into the prepared pie dish and bake for 25–30 minutes, or until golden.

To make the filling, beat the egg and sugar in a bowl until combined then add the flour and cornflour and beat until smooth. Warm the milk in a saucepan until almost boiling. Working quickly, over low–medium heat and stirring constantly, add the egg mixture to the milk and slowly bring to just below boiling point. This will take about 5 minutes and the mixture will thicken. Remove from the heat and add the butter and vanilla, stirring well.

Pour the filling through a strainer onto the prepared pie shell. Dust with the cinnamon and refrigerate to cool. Serve at room temperature.

Serves 8

Read Paula's story on page 16

RUTH GLICK

I came up with this recipe many years ago and thought it would make a wonderful cake for Passover. I've been making it for many years now, and it is loved by everyone.

Prune and chocolate cake

6 EGGS, SEPARATED

115 G (4 oz/½ CUP) CASTER
(SUPERFINE) SUGAR

250 G (9 oz) BEST-QUALITY DARK
CHOCOLATE, FINELY CHOPPED
OR GRATED

250 G (1 CUP, FIRMLY PACKED) PITTED
PRUNES, CHOPPED

PINCH OF SEA SALT

250 G (9 oz/2¾ CUPS) FINELY
GROUND WALNUTS

WHIPPED CREAM, TO SERVE

Preheat the oven to 180°C (350°F/Gas 4). Grease and line a 20 cm (8 inch) springform cake tin.

Beat the egg yolks and sugar (reserving 1 tablespoon for the egg whites) for several minutes until pale and well aerated. Gently fold in the chocolate and prunes.

Whisk the egg whites with the salt until soft peaks form. Add the reserved tablespoon of sugar and continue to whisk until firm peaks form. Fold the nuts into the egg whites as gently as possible until just combined.

Gently fold one large spoonful of the egg white mix into the egg yolk mix to soften it, then fold in the rest of the egg white mix. Pour into the prepared tin and bake for 50–60 minutes, or until golden brown and a skewer inserted into the middle comes out clean. Serve with whipped cream.

Serves 8

Photo on page 110

I immigrated to Perth with my parents in 1939 from Berlin. Every Sunday afternoon, without fail, my parents would gather with other German immigrants to discuss world events. There was always a cup of tea, a slice of wonderful cake and deep discussion. I especially remember my mother's apple cake, with a pastry lattice on top.

Cooking really wasn't on my agenda until after I got married, but I learned fast, living as a newlywed in London.

For many years we had a holiday house in the Margaret River region where we became really passionate about local produce and wines. My husband, Graham, spent balmy days fishing in his 'tinny' boat on Cowaramup Bay, catching herring and garfish. I learnt to cook herring 101 ways, and in the end Graham built his own hot and cold smokers, so the supply of herring became never ending!

Luckily for me, both my sons are fabulous cooks, and my daughter is a health fanatic, so we are very well looked after.

ESTHER WAKERMAN

I was born in Haifa, Israel, and arrived in Australia when I was five years old. My parents, originally from Romania, were Holocaust survivors. When the Communist government took over they escaped to Israel. Times were tough and work was hard to get, and so we decided to leave and start a new life in Australia.

Having grown up a 'princess' who never washed up or made a cup of coffee, it was a real shock to even think about cooking when I married. After a few tips from Mum, my first attempt was veal schnitzel and mashed potatoes. My new husband loved it – or at least he said he did! I was hooked; I loved looking through the Women's Weekly and Margaret Fulton cookbooks, making shopping lists and trying new recipes.

My mother, Shari, grew up with twelve siblings in a very observant family in the town of Satu Mare in Romania. She only finished six years of school and then stayed at home, helping with house duties and looking after the smaller children. She was an extraordinary cook and yet we never saw one recipe. Her food was rich, traditional Hungarian/Romanian comfort food – dishes full of flavour and texture, cooked and baked with love, enthusiasm and energy, which also describes her personality. I now cook many of her dishes and love retelling the stories of her famous dinners.

{Shari's cugloaf}

My mother Shari's wonderful cooking was known throughout the community, especially her amazing cugloaf. It became a tradition in our family to break the Yom Kippur fast with cugloaf at Nanna Shari's place, and since my parents passed away we have continued this tradition at our home; our children love it so much. It is so satisfying to see my family enjoying it with such relish, and I always feel my mother is looking down and smiling.

Shari's cugloaf

500 G (1 LB 2 OZ) CONTINENTAL
   FLOUR (ITALIAN 00 FLOUR)
35 G (1¼ OZ) FRESH YEAST
115 G (4 OZ/½ CUP) CASTER
   (SUPERFINE) SUGAR
100 ML (⅓ CUP PLUS 1 TABLESPOON)
   MILK
1 EGG
150 G (5½ OZ) SOUR CREAM
1 TABLESPOON VEGETABLE OIL
1 TEASPOON SALT
2 TABLESPOONS MILK MIXED
   WITH 60 ML (¼ CUP) HOT WATER
PLAIN (ALL-PURPOSE) FLOUR, FOR
   KNEADING
1 EGG, LIGHTLY BEATEN, FOR
   GLAZING

Place the continental (00) flour in a large bowl and make a well in the centre. Crumble the yeast into the well and sprinkle 1 tablespoon of the caster sugar on top of the yeast. Warm the milk and pour half over the yeast mixture. Leave for 5 minutes until the yeast starts to froth, then pour the remaining still-warm milk on top and set aside for 10 minutes, or until it froths again.

Break the egg into the well and add the sour cream, oil, remaining sugar, salt and half of the milk/water mixture. Mix until it forms a sticky dough.

Using the dough hook in an electric mixer, or by hand, knead for 10–15 minutes, adding the plain flour and milk/water as necessary to form a smooth elastic dough that comes away from the side of the bowl. Sprinkle with extra flour, cover with a tea towel (dish towel) and blanket and set aside in a warm place for 2 hours, or until well risen.

In the meantime, make the filling. Place all the filling ingredients in a bowl and mix with a wooden spoon until well combined and the consistency of a creamy icing.

Preheat the oven to 180°C (350°F/Gas 4). Butter a 32 x 22 cm (12¾ x 8½ inch) rectangular baking tin.

FILLING

375 G (13 OZ) **UNSALTED BUTTER,**
    AT ROOM TEMPERATURE
165 G (5¾ OZ/¾ CUP) **SUGAR**
300 G (10½ OZ) **DRINKING**
    CHOCOLATE

When the dough has risen, divide it into three balls. Each ball will make one cugloaf. Working individually, knead a ball on a well-floured board, then roll out until it is a very thin round, 40 cm (12–16 inches) in diameter.

Spread one-third of the chocolate filling right to the edge, completely covering the dough. Turn over the edge the whole way around to make a 1 cm (½ inch) border, then, starting at the side closest to you, roll up the pastry to make a long sausage or strudel shape. Place in the prepared tin, seam side down. The loaf can be squeezed in lengthways if necessary. Repeat with the other balls of dough and the remaining filling, laying them close together in the tin so the logs touch each other. Leave to rise for another half an hour or so.

Brush the logs with the egg wash and bake for 40 minutes, or until a dark golden brown colour and cooked through.

Leave to cool, then separate the logs. The cugloafs can be served one at a time. Any left-over loaves freeze well, wrapped individually in foil. Thaw at room temperature, then reheat in the oven, if preferred.

Makes 3 logs
Each log serves 10

Photo on page 145

HELEN SPICER

Born in Narol, Poland, in the 1930s, my childhood was not a good one. A year after the war broke out, my family and I were sent to a labour camp in Siberia for the duration of the war. When we were liberated and tried to leave Russia, we sat for many weeks at the train station in difficult and miserable conditions, before living in a refugee camp in Germany for five more difficult years.

In 1955, I moved to Australia, via a few years in San Francisco, where my sisters had already settled. Melbourne became my new home and I soon met and wed Jerry Spicer. We were blessed with four sons and our family is now complete with many grandchildren who live all over the world.

In my early years of married life, I admit to having many cooking disasters but, with perseverance and practice, baking became my specialty.

My mother, a very traditional Jewish cook, provided guidance with her motto; if you can't find the right ingredients it isn't worth making. Baking always reminds me of my mother as she also enjoyed it, especially traditional Jewish and European cakes and biscuits.

The first time I made rogala was by default. I planned on making a strudel but didn't have any apples, so I used only cinnamon and sultanas and made small rolls. Not satisfied with the result, I added jam and nuts and my rogala were created. My sons have grown up with the smells of my cooking, but my rogala is always the family favourite.

Rogala

225 G (8 OZ/1½ CUPS) PLAIN (ALL-PURPOSE) FLOUR

225 G (8 OZ/1½ CUPS) SELF-RAISING FLOUR

3 EGG YOLKS

115 G (4 OZ/½ CUP) CASTER (SUPERFINE) SUGAR

150 G (5½ OZ) SOUR CREAM

100 G (3½ OZ) UNSALTED BUTTER, AT ROOM TEMPERATURE

1 TEASPOON VANILLA EXTRACT

FILLING

175 G (½ CUP) CHOCOLATE HAZELNUT SPREAD

175 G (½ CUP) APRICOT JAM

60 G (½ CUP) ROUGHLY CHOPPED WALNUTS

80 G (½ CUP) FINELY CHOPPED MIXED DRIED FRUIT OR RAISINS

1 EGG WHITE, LIGHTLY WHISKED

110 G (½ CUP) SUGAR

Start this recipe the day before serving.

Place the flours in a large bowl and add the egg yolks, sugar, sour cream, butter and vanilla. Mix by hand until a soft dough forms. You can also make it in the food processor. Shape the dough into a log, cover with plastic wrap and refrigerate overnight.

Preheat the oven to 180°C (350°F/Gas 4). Line a baking tray.

Cut the dough into six pieces. Roll the first piece into a rectangle about 20 x 30 cm (8 x 12 inches). Spread on a light coating of chocolate hazelnut spread and jam. Sprinkle with some of the walnuts and dried fruit and roll into a firm roll, seam side down. Trim the ends and cut the roll into 8 even pieces. Brush the top of each piece with the egg white and then dip the top into the sugar. Place on the prepared tray, sugared side up. Repeat with the remaining pieces of dough. Bake for 30 minutes, or until golden.

Makes approximately 48 rogala

Feasting

Generous and abundant. Tables laden. I am always feeding people and the more the merrier, whether it's a small dinner party, a family celebration or a feast just for the pleasure of it. I love masses of flowers and candles to create an inviting and welcoming atmosphere. The turkey has roasted for hours, the skin is crisp, and the aroma intoxicating. Let the feast begin.

Paula x

Recipes

{Queen Elizabeth tart}

This is my take on the classic tuna tartare. It is a Sicilian-style dish that's great on a summer's day. Serve as a starter or, if having friends round, with pre-dinner drinks.

Tuna tartare

500 G (1 LB 2 OZ) RAW
    SASHIMI-GRADE TUNA
2 TABLESPOONS EXTRA VIRGIN
    OLIVE OIL
2 TABLESPOONS BABY CAPERS,
    RINSED AND DRAINED,
    ROUGHLY CHOPPED
5 SPRING ONIONS (SCALLIONS),
    FINELY CHOPPED
8–10 SICILIAN GREEN OLIVES,
    FINELY CHOPPED
1 TABLESPOON PINE NUTS,
    TOASTED AND CHOPPED
¼–½ TEASPOON DRIED CHILLI
    FLAKES, OR TO TASTE
SEA SALT AND FRESHLY GROUND
    BLACK PEPPER
LEMON JUICE, TO TASTE
SOURDOUGH TOASTS OR LAVASH
    OR FLATBREAD CRACKERS, FOR
    SERVING

Using a sharp knife, dice the tuna into 5 mm (¼ inch) squares.

Mix the tuna with the olive oil, capers, spring onion, olives, pine nuts and chilli flakes and season well with salt, pepper and a little lemon juice. Drizzle with extra olive oil to serve.

Serve immediately with the sourdough toasts or crackers.

Serves 8–10 with drinks

Family and friends, drinking and eating, fun and laughter are what I do best.

I come from a long line of cooks and entertainers – my two grandmothers, mother and aunts in South Africa all loved to create recipes and entertained continuously. I didn't help much in the kitchen – I think I was too naughty to be let in. We lived right on the beach, so there was abundant seafood and of course (being South African) lots of meat. In the 1960s my aunt wrote a cookbook called What's Cooking? *to raise money for Glendale, a home for the handicapped, so contributing a recipe to this book continues a family tradition.*

I have more time now the kids have grown up and with my support team – my wife, Shirley – I have moved from the barbecue to the kitchen. I find it relaxing and therapeutic to create food my family loves. My motto is family and friends teamed with good food and wine creates much laughter and a great evening.

ERWIN JEREMIAH

My mom took great pride in her cooking, bustling about the kitchen preparing lunches and dinners with me by her side, slicing, peeling and pounding. She is of Chinese descent and when she married my dad, who is a mix of Portuguese, Swiss and Indonesian, his love of curry and spicy food was unfamiliar. Through determination and with guidance, she soon mastered the art of making excellent Malaysian Portuguese dishes.

I grew up around the aromatic smell of spices. I started cooking when I was young, under my mom's supervision, preparing basic dishes like fried fish and nasi goreng. The real adventure began when I left home, wanting to impress my friends with authentic home-cooked meals. There were many calls to home and my housemates were delighted to be my guinea pigs.

After leaving university, I never stopped cooking and entertaining. I moved to Sydney in 2008 to pursue a PhD in hydrology, and continued to share my passion for cooking with many friends and later, my partner and greatest fan.

In my mom's kitchen, this dish was served for special occasions and festivals. I always knew I was in for a treat when she asked me to cut some banana leaves from our backyard tree. Don't be daunted by the number of ingredients in this spice paste. The results are well worth it. It can be made a couple of days ahead and stored in the fridge.

Malaysian barramundi

7–10 DRIED RED CHILLIES OR 2 TABLESPOONS MILD RED CHILLI PASTE

5 CM (2 INCH) PIECE GALANGAL (OR SUBSTITUTE WITH EXTRA GINGER), PEELED AND THINLY SLICED

5 CM (2 INCH) PIECE FRESH TURMERIC, PEELED AND THINLY SLICED, OR 3 TEASPOONS GROUND TURMERIC

2 TABLESPOONS FINELY GRATED FRESH GINGER

2 LEMONGRASS STEMS, WHITE PART ONLY, THINLY SLICED, OR 2 TABLESPOONS LEMONGRASS PASTE

1 LARGE RED ONION, ROUGHLY CHOPPED

2 CLOVES GARLIC, PEELED

500 ML (2 CUPS) COCONUT MILK

1 TABLESPOON VEGETABLE OIL

½ TEASPOON SUGAR

1 TEASPOON WHITE VINEGAR

1 TEASPOON LEMON JUICE

½ TEASPOON SEA SALT

FRESHLY GROUND BLACK PEPPER

4 BANANA LEAVES (OPTIONAL)

8 x 200 G (7 OZ) BARRAMUNDI FILLETS

8 KAFFIR LIME LEAVES, STEM REMOVED, FINELY SHREDDED

Halve the dried chillies (if using) and soak in hot water for 5 minutes. Put the galangal, turmeric, ginger and lemongrass in a blender with the onion and garlic. Drain the chillies, squeeze out the excess water, remove and discard the seeds (if you prefer less heat) and add to the blender. Pour in 1 cup of the coconut milk and blend until it is a fine paste.

Heat the oil in a wok or large frying pan over medium–high heat. Pour the spice paste into the pan and sauté until the oil separates and floats, about 10 minutes. Stir in the rest of the coconut milk, then the sugar, vinegar, lemon juice, salt and pepper. There should be a balance between sweet, sour and salty. Simmer, stirring from time to time, until reduced by half and a thick paste forms, about 30 minutes. Allow to cool before using, or refrigerate for several days until needed.

Preheat the oven to 180°C (350°F/Gas 4).

If using the banana leaves, cut to the right size so they are sufficiently large enough to wrap each fish fillet into a parcel. Alternatively, you will need 8 pieces of baking paper, each large enough to wrap one fillet of fish. You will also need 8 slightly larger sheets of foil.

Spread 1 tablespoon of the spice paste on one side of a fish fillet. Sprinkle half a shredded kaffir lime leaf on the banana leaf/baking paper and place the fish on top, paste side down. Spread another spoon of the paste on top of the fish and sprinkle with another half of a shredded lime leaf. Folding the banana leaf/baking paper first, wrap the fish in a neat parcel. Then wrap in the foil to encase the parcel, ensuring the edges are well sealed. Repeat with the remaining fish fillets.

Place the fish parcels on a baking tray and bake for 20–25 minutes, or until the fish is just cooked through. Allow to rest for 10 minutes before serving and opening the packages.

Serves 8

LISA BRECKLER

This recipe has become a family Shabbat favourite. When my children were young they didn't like fish so I invented the name 'fish crumble' to make the dish sound fun! As they grew up, I experimented with different herbs and types of bread. A slightly stale loaf makes the crumb topping very crunchy. This dish works just as well with any whole fish or fillets.

Salmon crumble

1 SIDE OF SALMON, ABOUT 1 KG
   (2 LB 4 OZ), SKINNED AND PIN-
   BONED
1 LEMON, SLICED
180 ML (¾ CUP) VERJUICE
1 TABLESPOON OLIVE OIL, FOR
   DRIZZLING

CRUMBLE
3 CLOVES GARLIC
1 LONG RED CHILLI, DESEEDED
1 LARGE HANDFUL DILL FRONDS
1 LARGE HANDFUL FLAT-LEAF
   (ITALIAN) PARSLEY LEAVES
1 LARGE HANDFUL BASIL LEAVES
120 G (4¼ OZ) SOURDOUGH BREAD,
   NO CRUSTS
JUICE OF 1 LEMON
60 ML (¼ CUP) OLIVE OIL
1 TEASPOON SEA SALT
FRESHLY GROUND BLACK PEPPER

Preheat the oven to 180°C (350°F/Gas 4).

Place the fish in a roasting tin and lay the lemon slices around the fish.

Put the crumble ingredients in a food processor and process until the mixture forms a coarse crumb texture and is well combined.

Press the crumb mixture firmly onto the fish. Pour the verjuice around the fish, on top of the lemon slices. Drizzle the olive oil over the fish, place in the oven and bake for 15 minutes (rare) to 30 minutes (well done), or until cooked to your liking. Remove from the oven and loosely cover with foil for at least 15 minutes to rest, before serving. Serve warm or at room temperature.

Serves 6

I grew up in the tiny Jewish community of Auckland, New Zealand. We managed to keep a traditional Jewish home and my father, a paediatrician, was the mohel for the whole country.

Our family often visited Fiji and Rarotonga so my father could immunise children. I remember the exotic food and fascinating cultures. Dad and I used to spend time together fishing and then devising wonderful ways to cook the fish we caught.

My mother's family was in Melbourne so we moved here in 1982. It was fantastic to suddenly be connected to a large extended family and to this day, we all still meet for very large Seders and Rosh Hashanah celebrations. I imagine my late grandparents, who fled Poland with my mother when she was just nine months old, would be so proud to see such a large and loving group of almost 50 around the table. There is always an abundance of beautiful food and much discussion.

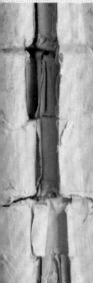

ROBIN SOBEL

I was born into a family that ate canned soup, tinned fruit and processed food. How things have changed.

Before my wife, Marylou, and I first immigrated to Australia from South Africa we had some basic cooking lessons, but once I was settled in Sydney and had three young daughters, I found I was too busy to keep it up. I started cooking again about five years ago, as it gave me a new way to be creative.

My cooking is simple; I always start from scratch with quality ingredients, fresh herbs and spices, using recipes only as a guide. If it doesn't work out, I try again with a different combination of flavours. My family are my best critics.

Friends think Marylou is so fortunate because she doesn't have to cook but I think I am the lucky one because I love it so much. No one bothers me when I am in the kitchen, so it is my time out and while everyone else is asleep I quietly research new recipes. The biggest thrill for me is watching my family and friends enjoy my creations, especially when they think I have slaved away in the kitchen all day. Little do they know what a pleasure it has been! (See also Robin's osso buco with lentils on page 128.)

{Herb-crusted lamb rack}

This is probably my favourite go-to meal when I need to make a simple yet delicious dinner. It is always perfect, will impress most guests and my family never gets tired of the lamb. If you're in a rush, skip the overnight marinating, just give it a quick brown in a pan, then roast in the oven.

Herb-crusted lamb racks

180 ML (¾ CUP) VEGETABLE OIL

2 RACKS OF LAMB, FRENCH TRIMMED

MARINADE

1 BUNCH MINT

1 BUNCH CORIANDER (CILANTRO)

4 ROSEMARY SPRIGS, LEAVES PICKED

1 BUNCH FLAT-LEAF (ITALIAN) PARSLEY

4 CLOVES GARLIC, PEELED

1 TEASPOON FINELY GRATED FRESH GINGER

1 TABLESPOON GROUND CUMIN

2 TABLESPOONS SOY SAUCE

2 TABLESPOONS RED WINE VINEGAR

1 LONG RED CHILLI, CHOPPED

1 TEASPOON SEA SALT

FRESHLY GROUND BLACK PEPPER

If possible, start this recipe the day before serving.

Place all the marinade ingredients in a blender with half the oil. Blend together, then slowly add enough of the remaining oil until it becomes a thick spreadable paste.

Put the lamb into a non-reactive bowl and coat evenly with the marinade. Place in the fridge for several hours to marinate, or preferably overnight.

When ready to cook, remove the meat from the fridge and allow to come to room temperature.

Preheat the oven to 220°C (425°F/Gas 7).

Heat a large roasting tin or an ovenproof non-stick frying pan over high heat. Add a splash of oil and, when hot, sear the lamb for a couple of minutes on all sides until well browned. You may need to scrape up some of the marinade from the pan and put it back on top of the lamb.

Place in the oven and roast for 12 minutes (rare) to 15 minutes (medium). Transfer the lamb to a platter and rest for 5–10 minutes, loosely covered with foil.

Slice into 2-bone portions to serve. Serve with smashed potatoes (page 87) and a green salad.

Serves 6

Photo on page 161

My mother-in-law, Violet, brought many rice-based recipes to Australia from her native Baghdad via Israel. Her standard was tomato basmati rice, which my family has always devoured. I have modified the recipe so it can also be made with turmeric, which is so popular and perfect alongside a curry or other spiced dish.

Yellow rice

1 TABLESPOON OLIVE OIL
1 SMALL ONION, FINELY CHOPPED
FRESHLY GROUND BLACK PEPPER
½ TEASPOON GROUND TURMERIC
220 G (1 CUP) BASMATI RICE, WELL
   RINSED
375 ML (1½ CUPS) CHICKEN STOCK
SALT

Choose a medium-sized saucepan that has a firm-fitting lid. Heat the olive oil over medium heat and fry the onion until soft and translucent, about 15 minutes. Add the pepper and turmeric and cook until fragrant, then add the rice and stir until well coated with the onion mix.

Add the stock to the pan and bring to the boil. Add salt to taste. Cover, reduce the heat to low and cook for 15 minutes. Avoid taking the lid off the pan so the rice steams and does not dry out. Serve immediately.

Serves 4

VARIATION: For tomato basmati rice, replace the turmeric with 1 heaped tablespoon tomato paste (concentrated purée).

Photo on page 167
Read Shereen's story on page 210

REUBEN SOLOMON

Reuben and his brothers trekked from their home town of Rangoon, Burma, to the safety of India, mere steps ahead of the Japanese bombing in 1943. Later he travelled to London, then Sri Lanka, where he met and wed Charmaine, before migrating with their daughters to Sydney in 1959.

Gifted with perfect pitch, Reuben initially taught himself to play clarinet by listening to recordings of Artie Shaw and Benny Goodman, eventually playing both classical and jazz. His ability to improvise crossed over into the kitchen – his cooking quite often had elements of the unexpected. He was always quite at home in the kitchen. Both he and Charmaine loved the exotic food they left behind and since Sydney in the late 1950s offered no other options, they learned to cook it for themselves. Ingredients were hard to come by and from time to time exotic spices and curry powders, together with pages of handwritten recipes, would arrive from Charmaine's mother and aunts in Colombo.

Reuben faithfully recreated his much-loved Burmese dishes. One, balachaung, was so laden with garlic and dried shrimp that, despite cooking it in the garage, his daughters could smell it half a block away as they walked home from school. Charmaine moved from journalism to writing best-selling cookbooks – a formidable 31 titles.

Charmaine and Reuben would move around the kitchen happily cooking and singing together, creating Sunday lunch jam sessions that lasted well past dinnertime for musician friends and relatives. When Reuben passed away in 2009, it marked the end of a very special era.

One day many years ago, Charmaine was at work and Reuben was minding their three young children. He took them on an excursion to the Roselands shopping centre, entered into a cooking competition and created this masterpiece on stage – the only fellow among a flurry of aproned women. Although not the winning recipe, Charmaine's cousin Peggy loved it so much she cooked it for her daughter's wedding lunch.

Chicken Everest

1 x 1.5 KG (3 LB 5 OZ) CHICKEN

PASTE
2 CLOVES GARLIC, CRUSHED
2 TEASPOONS FINELY GRATED
   FRESH GINGER
1½ TABLESPOONS CURRY POWDER
1 TEASPOON SWEET PAPRIKA
2 TEASPOONS SALT
½ TEASPOON FRESHLY GROUND
   BLACK PEPPER
1 TEASPOON GARAM MASALA
2 TABLESPOONS LEMON JUICE
10 FRESH CURRY LEAVES
2 TEASPOONS LIGHT SOY SAUCE
2 TABLESPOONS VEGETABLE OIL
2 TABLESPOONS GROUND RICE
3 SPRING ONIONS (SCALLIONS),
   CHOPPED
1 SMALL HANDFUL CORIANDER
   (CILANTRO) LEAVES, PLUS EXTRA,
   FOR GARNISH

Put the paste ingredients into a food processor and process to make a paste. Add a little warm water, if necessary, to reach a spreading consistency.

Rub the inside and outside of the chicken with the paste, carefully sliding some under the skin on the breast. Place in the fridge and marinate for at least 1 hour.

Preheat the oven to 170°C (325°F/Gas 3).

Place the chicken in an oiled roasting dish and roast, uncovered, for 1¼ hours, or until golden brown and the juices run clear when the thigh is pierced with a knife. If the chicken browns too much during cooking, cover with foil. Remove from the oven and rest for 15 minutes, loosely covered with foil.

Garnish with the extra coriander leaves. Serve warm or at room temperature with yellow rice (page 163) and a salad.

Serves 4–6

My mother often served duck on special occasions and I think of her whenever I make it. Steaming the duck in this recipe renders down most of the fat and the Asian sauce gives it a modern element. It's a lovely way to cook duck or chicken, in fact.

Glazed Asian duck

250 ML (1 CUP) VEGETARIAN OYSTER SAUCE

250 ML (1 CUP) KECAP MANIS

260 G (¾ CUP) GOLDEN SYRUP (LIGHT TREACLE) OR 165 G (¾ CUP, FIRMLY PACKED) BROWN SUGAR

2 TEASPOONS GROUND CINNAMON

1 TEASPOON CHINESE FIVE SPICE

4 STAR ANISE

8–12 DUCK MARYLANDS (LEG QUARTERS)

If possible, start this recipe the day before serving.

Combine all the ingredients (except the duck) in a saucepan and bring to the boil. Allow to cool. Trim the duck of excess fat, wash and pat dry. Place in a non-reactive bowl and refrigerate until needed.

When the marinade is cool, pour over the duck legs, cover and refrigerate for at least 6 hours, or overnight.

Remove the duck from the marinade, reserving the liquid. Prick the skin of the duck with a fork to release excess fat when cooking. Lay the duck in a single layer in a bamboo steamer, place over a large saucepan of simmering water (or use a wok with a steamer plate), cover with a tight-fitting lid and steam for 1 hour. This process can be done several hours ahead.

Preheat the oven to 180°C (350°F/Gas 4). Line a large baking tray.

Remove the duck from the steamer and place on the prepared tray. Brush with the reserved marinade and bake, basting with the reserved marinade from time to time, for 30–45 minutes until the skin is crisp and deep brown. If the duck is browning too quickly, reduce the temperature to 160°C (315°F/Gas 2–3) for the remaining cooking time. Serve with steamed rice and bok choy.

Serves 8–12

My grandmother was the most amazing self-taught cook. Every Friday she would arrive at our home to stay the weekend, and I was always her assistant when she made fresh apple strudel, pulling the pastry on the dining room table. My Viennese father and Polish mother, as immigrants to a new country, both worked long hours. As a ten-year-old, to the delighted surprise of my exhausted mother, I would make dinner for the family. That's where my love of cooking started.

Our home was always open to anyone. The fridge was always fully loaded with food, as my mother worked in a deli and would bring home all my favourites. My grandmother made schnitzel and potato salad every Saturday night. Our table was always overflowing. Today, nothing gives me greater pleasure than to do the same; fill our home with family, friends and groaning tables.

JANETTE KORNHAUSER

My husband and I moved to the Gold Coast from Melbourne in 1983, one year after we married. We were both from Polish families (as well as English on my side) and big family dinners were an integral part of our lives.

I grew up in a home where dinner was always a three-course meal. My mum, Shirley, is still a renowned and fabulous cook. She learned most of her European cooking from my paternal grandmother, Baba, who lived with us until she passed away. I remember fondly when Baba made kreplach *with me – many years later my mum sat with my daughters doing the same.*

Food on the Gold Coast back in the early days was neither continental nor interesting. It became more meaningful to make food from home and cooking cured feelings of homesickness. I returned from trips to Melbourne weighed down with bags full of treasures from delicatessens, butchers and bakeries and still today I bring back bagel and onion roll supplies. But my real passion for cooking began some 25 years ago when my husband became a vegetarian.

Living in a very small Jewish community, I always felt it important to make a fuss of Shabbat dinner and yomtovim, and often invited other families, who like us did not have their relatives around. These friends became our family. A true joy, our three daughters still get excited to see what's on the menu and I feel their pride when they invite friends to our table.

Trying to find a vegetarian dish that can be both a hearty stand-alone meal or a great side dish is always a challenge. This brown rice and vegetable dish is very filling, interesting and colourful. My family loves this dish and it goes beautifully with the maple and orange-glazed turkey (page 172) – almost like a great stuffing served on the side. It also works well with risoni or couscous and during Passover I substitute quinoa for the rice.

Warm brown rice salad

400 G (2 CUPS) BROWN RICE

1 LITRE (4 CUPS) WATER

1 TEASPOON SALT

2 ZUCCHINIS (COURGETTES)

1 EGGPLANT (AUBERGINE)

1 RED ONION, PEELED

1 PARSNIP, PEELED

1 SWEET POTATO, SKIN ON

1 CARROT, PEELED

500 G (1 LB 2 OZ) CHERRY
   TOMATOES, HALVED

SEA SALT AND FRESHLY GROUND
   BLACK PEPPER

125 ML (½ CUP) OLIVE OIL

80 G (½ CUP) SULTANAS
   (GOLDEN RAISINS)

45 G (¼ CUP) DRIED CRANBERRIES

50 G (⅓ CUP) PINE NUTS, TOASTED

1 HANDFUL CHOPPED FLAT-LEAF
   (ITALIAN) PARSLEY

1 SMALL HANDFUL CHOPPED MINT
   LEAVES

1 TABLESPOON ZA'ATAR, OR TO
   TASTE (SEE NOTE)

Put the rice, water and salt into a saucepan. Bring to the boil, reduce to a simmer and cover with a lid until cooked, about 40 minutes. Alternatively, cook the rice in a rice cooker.

Preheat the oven to 200°C (400°F/Gas 6). Line a large baking tray.

Cut the vegetables into 1 cm (½ inch) cubes and place all the vegetables and the tomatoes on the prepared tray. Season well with salt and pepper and drizzle generously with the olive oil. (The juices of the oil and tomatoes make the dressing when mixed with the rice.) Roast for 30 minutes, tossing from time to time, until the vegetables are browned at the edges and cooked.

As soon as the rice is cooked, mix in the sultanas and cranberries and allow to stand for a few minutes. Toss with the roasted vegetables, pine nuts, parsley, mint and za'atar. Season with more salt and pepper to taste.

Serve warm or at room temperature.

Serves 10–12

NOTE: Za'atar is a Middle Eastern spice mix made from dried herbs mixed with sesame seeds, sumac and often salt. It is available from spice stores and good delicatessens.

My turkey recipe evolved from necessity of feeding large numbers. The maple and orange glaze was something I came across in my travels, and with constant basting, it results in a fantastic juicy meat that is not too sweet, with just a good hint of citrus.

Maple and orange-glazed turkey

1 RED APPLE, PEELED

1 x 5 KG (11 LB) TURKEY

80 ML (⅓ CUP) OLIVE OIL

SEA SALT

2 CLOVES GARLIC, CRUSHED

ZEST OF 1 ORANGE, REMOVED IN
   WIDE STRIPS

125 ML (½ CUP) PURE MAPLE SYRUP

125 ML (½ CUP) FRESHLY SQUEEZED
   ORANGE JUICE

500 ML (2 CUPS) CHICKEN STOCK

You will need a roasting tin large enough to hold the turkey.

Preheat the oven to 200°C (400°F/Gas 6).

Stuff the apple into the turkey's cavity. Tie the legs together with kitchen string. Rub the turkey all over with the oil, salt, garlic and orange zest. Put the turkey, breast side up, in the roasting tin and roast for 30 minutes.

Meanwhile, in a bowl, mix the maple syrup, orange juice and 1 cup of the chicken stock. Remove 1 cup of the maple syrup mix, add the remaining stock to the bowl and reserve for basting.

After 30 minutes of roasting, pour the maple syrup mix over the turkey, and cover the whole tin with foil. Reduce the oven temperature to 170°C (325°F/Gas 3) and roast the turkey for a further 2½–3 hours, basting generously every 30 minutes with the reserved basting mix.

For the last 30 minutes, remove the foil and roast the turkey until it is brown and crisp. Prick the thigh to see if the juices run clear. If they are pink, the turkey is not cooked enough. Return to the oven until cooked. Remove the turkey from the tin and set aside to rest, covered with foil, for 20–30 minutes.

Pour all the pan juices and any left-over basting mix into a small saucepan. Skim off and discard any oil and scum. Bring to the boil and simmer for 15 minutes, or until a glossy glaze forms.

Pour the glaze over the turkey, reserving some to serve on the side. Serve with warm brown rice salad (page 171).

Serves 8–10

My whole style of cooking changed when I converted to Judaism because of the kashrut laws. This recipe is the result of that. I really loved the creamy potato bakes I grew up eating, but I didn't want to mix meat and milk, so the recipe needed to change. After searching and experimenting for some time, I finally adapted a potato gratin into this recipe.

Potato and onion gratin

80 ML (⅓ CUP) OLIVE OIL

2 LARGE ONIONS, HALVED AND
    THINLY SLICED

1 TEASPOON CHOPPED THYME OR
    ROSEMARY LEAVES

800 G (1 LB 14 OZ) WAXY POTATOES,
    SLICED

SEA SALT AND FRESHLY GROUND
    BLACK PEPPER

250 ML (1 CUP) CHICKEN STOCK

Preheat the oven to 180°C (350°F/Gas 4). Grease a 1.5 litre (6 cup) gratin dish or shallow ovenproof dish.

Heat the oil in a saucepan over medium heat. Add the onion and cook for 20 minutes, or until soft and golden brown, stirring occasionally. Remove from the heat and stir in the thyme or rosemary.

Arrange one-third of the potato in the prepared dish, top with one-third of the onion and season with salt and pepper. Repeat with two more layers, finishing with the onion. Gently pour the stock over the top of the potato and onion, until just covered. Cover with foil and bake for 1 hour. Remove the foil and bake for a further 15–20 minutes, or until golden brown.

Serves 8

I was born in Adelaide to Australian, non-Jewish parents. I met my husband, Eric, over 30 years ago, and we moved to Perth. I quickly blended into the Jewish way of life with Eric's family, and the togetherness I felt at weekly Shabbat meals was something I cherished.

A few years later, Eric and I moved to an island off the north Queensland coast to live for six years. We owned a restaurant there, which certainly developed my cooking skills, even though I had been cooking with my grandmother from a young age. There were no Jewish residents on the island and we particularly missed Eric's family during the chagim. I purchased a Jewish cookbook and my mother-in-law posted me ingredients like matzo meal so I could cook the dishes that Eric loved. I remember spending hours preparing for the chagim, cooking the customary dishes that Eric missed so much. He was overwhelmed when he came home to the familiar smells of his upbringing.

I have warm memories of cooking with my grandmother, who lived with us, and with my late mother and mother-in-law. Today I love experimenting with recipes when entertaining. Much to my best friend's horror, I like to use my guests as taste testers.

This dish is a pretty easy recipe which can be prepared ahead and cooked at the last minute. It came about as a result of not wanting to make fritters but really needing a deliciously satisfying zucchini dish.

Zucchini and gruyère gratin

60 ML (¼ CUP) EXTRA VIRGIN
OLIVE OIL, PLUS EXTRA, FOR
DRIZZLING

600 G (1 LB 5 OZ) ZUCCHINIS
(COURGETTES), SLICED INTO THIN
ROUNDS

2 CLOVES GARLIC, CRUSHED

2 PINCHES OF FRESHLY GRATED
NUTMEG

SEA SALT AND FRESHLY GROUND
BLACK PEPPER

1 ONION, CHOPPED

2 X 400 G (14 OZ) TINS WHOLE
TOMATOES, DRAINED AND
CHOPPED

60 ML (¼ CUP) VERJUICE

6 FRESH OR 3 DRIED BAY LEAVES

100 G (1 CUP) GRATED GRUYÈRE
CHEESE

15 G (¼ CUP) FRESH BREADCRUMBS

25 G (¼ CUP) GRATED PARMESAN
CHEESE

Preheat the oven to 180°C (350°F/Gas 4). Grease a 1.5 litre (6 cup) ovenproof dish.

Heat half of the olive oil in a frying pan and cook the zucchini over low heat for 5 minutes until starting to soften. Stir in the garlic and cook for 1–2 minutes. Add the nutmeg and salt and pepper, then transfer to the ovenproof dish.

Heat the rest of the oil in the pan and cook the onion until soft, about 15 minutes. Add the tomatoes, verjuice and bay leaves and cook until the sauce is thick and the liquid is almost evaporated, stirring regularly. Season well and remove the bay leaves.

Sprinkle the gruyère cheese on the zucchini, then spread the tomato sauce on top. Mix the breadcrumbs and parmesan together, sprinkle over the tomato sauce and drizzle with a little olive oil. Bake for 20–25 minutes, or until golden.

Serves 8 as a side dish

I was a 1980 Bondi baby. I swam before I could walk and spent my days wandering the beach.

I learned to cook mostly from my mum and my nana. My mum is an adventurous cook, rarely paying attention to timing or quantities, her food always erratic and delicious. Nana was a precise baker and I don't ever remember her presenting a cake that hadn't risen beautifully. The first dish I learned to make was pancakes, and from the age of six I would take orders and serve my family breakfast in bed. I loved those mornings, the sound of frying butter in the pan harmonious with the gorgeous smells wafting through the house. Later, I paid attention to cookbooks, recipes from anywhere at all, Shabbat table discussions, Iain Hewitson and Peter Russell-Clarke on TV.

I have a great passion for food and cooking, particularly food that nourishes both the body and soul.

As a kid I used to hate eating mandarins at recess and built up a mound in my school locker. By the end of the year my rotting collection not only ruined my maths notes but had friends complaining as well. Years later, I ate some really good mandarin shortbread at a café and started to change my mandarin attitude. I came to see that mandarins were wonderful when cooked and a great substitute for other citrus in desserts. And just like that, my mandarin puddings were born. This pudding is perfect for impressive entertaining as it can be prepared a couple of hours in advance, ready to bake in the ramekins.

Mandarin delicious puddings

50 G (1¾ oz) **BUTTER, AT ROOM TEMPERATURE**

100 G (3½ oz) **CASTER** (SUPERFINE) **SUGAR**

2 TEASPOONS FINELY GRATED MANDARIN ZEST

2 EGGS, SEPARATED

50 G (1¾ oz/⅓ CUP) **SELF-RAISING FLOUR**

200 ML (¾ CUP PLUS 1 TABLESPOON) **MILK**

80 ML (⅓ CUP) **MANDARIN JUICE**

CREAM OR ICE CREAM, TO SERVE

Preheat the oven to 180°C (350°F/Gas 4). Butter four 250 ml (1 cup) capacity ovenproof ramekins.

Using an electric mixer, beat the butter, sugar and mandarin zest until pale, light and fluffy. Add the egg yolks, one at a time, beating well after each addition, then add the flour and mix until well combined. Stir in the milk and juice. Don't worry if the mixture looks curdled; it will come together.

In a separate bowl, whisk the egg whites until stiff but not dry, then fold into the batter using a large metal spoon.

Pour into the prepared ramekins, then place them in an ovenproof dish. Pour boiling water into the dish until it comes halfway up the sides of the ramekins. Bake for 40 minutes, or until the puddings are puffed and golden. Serve immediately with cream or ice cream.

Serves 4

A good crème caramel must have the perfect colour and the custard must be perfectly smooth with no bubbles. Luckily, it can be prepared a day or two before it is needed, and must be refrigerated at least 12 hours before serving.

Crème caramel

CARAMEL
250 ML (1 CUP) WATER
440 G (2 CUPS) SUGAR

CUSTARD
8 EGGS
165 G (¾ CUP) SUGAR
2 TEASPOONS VANILLA EXTRACT
1 LITRE (4 CUPS) MILK

Start this recipe the day before serving.

You will need a 2 litre (8 cup) shallow ovenproof dish, a larger ovenproof dish to use as a bain-marie (water bath) and a serving plate with a rim to catch the caramel.

Preheat the oven to 150°C (300°F/Gas 2).

To make the caramel, place the water and sugar in a saucepan and bring to a boil. Continue to cook on a steady boil until the syrup starts to change to a deep golden caramel. This can take up to 20 minutes. Do not stir, just tilt the saucepan around to ensure there is even heat. Carefully remove from the heat – it will continue to cook. Pour immediately into the shallow ovenproof dish, swirling it around the base and up the sides. Set aside.

To make the custard, using a hand whisk (to avoid bubbles), lightly whisk the eggs with the sugar and vanilla until the sugar is dissolved. Add the milk and continue to whisk until well combined. Strain the liquid into a jug to remove any bubbles, which can affect the custard's smoothness. Pour into the dish, on top of the caramel.

Sit the crème caramel in the larger ovenproof dish and fill with water to nearly halfway up the side of the crème caramel dish. Bake for 1 hour until the top of the custard feels just set but has a bit of a wobble. Remove from the oven, carefully take the dish out of the water and place on a wire rack to cool, then refrigerate overnight.

To turn the crème caramel out before serving, run a knife around the rim to loosen the side, then invert onto the serving plate.

Serves 10–12

NOTE: For individual serves, use ten ¾-cup ramekins.

JOYCE HASSAN

My French-speaking parents arrived in Adelaide from Alexandria in 1950. Many Egyptian Jews came to South Australia at that time, and the small community they formed began to thrive. My husband, Alfred, also comes from Egypt, and we share the same exotic culinary background and tastes here in Adelaide.

My interest in cooking began at a young age, looking over my mother's shoulder as she prepared many grand, bountiful and labour-intensive meals. I realised the best way to learn her cooking style was to give a helping hand and listen carefully to tips. When I baked with her, she would tell me to 'feel the pastry' to work out what it needed. Her recipes were never exact – and for me, it has always been 'a little of this' and 'as much as it takes'.

NAOMI ALTHAUS

One of my early memories is of my mother and grandmother preparing for Passover in the outside kitchen, a remnant from the old Hungarian style of having two kitchens, which allowed for the really messy cooking to be done out of the house. My siblings and I would play in the garden with the most amazing smells around us.

Growing up, everything took place in the kitchen. It's where stories were told, decisions were made, children nurtured and family bonds cemented. We were always being fed – not just our bodies, but our hearts and souls.

My mother, Eva, ran a successful catering business and she passed her skills on to me. After five years of travelling and collecting tastes from around the world, I returned to Melbourne and started a small boutique catering company.

It gives me great pleasure to know that my food helps families sit round the table, share food and enjoy being together, creating their own memories from the food they are enjoying.

A few years after starting my business, I married and we now have three children, who are by far my toughest customers. Like the generation before me, I am happiest when we are all sharing good times, eating and talking like there is no tomorrow.

{Lemon tart}

This is a simply wonderful lemon tart, as perfect for dessert as afternoon tea. My original recipe, which works very well, is with margarine instead of butter so it can be pareve and part of a meat meal.

Lemon tart

PASTRY

220 G (7¾ OZ) UNSALTED BUTTER,
    AT ROOM TEMPERATURE
120 G (4¼ OZ/¾ CUP) ICING
    (CONFECTIONERS') SUGAR
2 EGG YOLKS
340 G (12 OZ/2⅓ SCANT CUPS) PLAIN
    (ALL-PURPOSE) FLOUR

FILLING

450 ML (1¾ CUPS) FRESHLY
    SQUEEZED LEMON JUICE,
    STRAINED
375 G (13 OZ/1⅔ CUPS) CASTER
    (SUPERFINE) SUGAR
9 EGGS

You will need a 30 cm (12 inch) tart (flan) tin with a removable base.

For the pastry, cream the butter and sugar in an electric mixer until pale and creamy. Add the egg yolks and beat until combined. Mix in the flour by hand. Alternatively, place all the ingredients in a food processor and process until a ball of dough forms.

Place spoonfuls of the dough in the prepared tin and press in with your fingers to form the pastry shell. Reserve a small amount of dough for patching cracks, if needed later. Line the pastry shell with foil, pressing into the edge of the base and making sure the sides are covered, then place in the fridge for at least 4 hours.

Preheat the oven to 160°C (315°F/Gas 2–3).

Fill the foil-lined pastry shell with baking weights or dried beans and blind bake for 15–20 minutes, until no longer raw. Remove the weights and foil carefully, patch any cracks with the reserved dough, and bake for a further 15 minutes, or until the pastry is golden and cooked through.

For the filling, lightly whisk (to avoid bubbles) the lemon juice, sugar and eggs together, making sure the sugar dissolves.

Strain the filling into a jug to remove any bubbles, then pour into the pastry shell. Bake for 30 minutes, or until the mixture is almost set, with a slight wobble.

Serve at room temperature.

Serves 12–16

Photo on page 183

This recipe came from Pauline Bloomhill and was an old favourite served at all bar mitzvah brochas *at the Bulawayo synagogue, catered for by WIZO ladies. Guests were always flocking to get a slice and as a young child I remember only ever managing to get a few crumbs. After many years Pauline decided it was time to share the recipe with her friends so that they could continue her legacy, and the recipe was later sold as a fundraiser.*

Queen Elizabeth tart

250 G (1½ CUPS) DATES, PITTED AND
    CHOPPED
75 G (½ CUP) PECANS, CHOPPED
1 TEASPOON BICARBONATE OF
    SODA (BAKING SODA)
250 ML (1 CUP) BOILING WATER
60 G (2¼ OZ) UNSALTED BUTTER, AT
    ROOM TEMPERATURE
220 G (7¾ OZ/1 CUP) SUGAR
1 EGG
¼ TEASPOON SALT
1 TEASPOON VANILLA EXTRACT
225 G (8 OZ/1½ CUPS) PLAIN (ALL-
    PURPOSE) FLOUR
1 TEASPOON BAKING POWDER

TOPPING
150 G (¾ CUP, LIGHTLY PACKED) DARK
    BROWN SUGAR
90 G (3¼ OZ) UNSALTED BUTTER
35 G (½ CUP) SHREDDED COCONUT
140 ML (½ CUP PLUS 1 TABLESPOON)
    PURE CREAM (35% FAT)

Preheat the oven to 180°C (350°F/Gas 4). Grease a 28–30 cm (11–12 inch) tart (flan) tin with a removable base.

Place the dates and nuts in a small bowl. Mix in the bicarbonate of soda, then pour on the boiling water. Leave to stand.

Cream the butter and sugar in an electric mixer. Add the egg, salt and vanilla and mix well.

Sift the flour and baking powder together, then add to the egg mixture on low speed. Fold in the date and pecan mix with a large spoon. Pour into the prepared tin and bake for 30–40 minutes, or until golden and cooked through.

Meanwhile, combine all the ingredients for the topping in a saucepan and bring to the boil. Simmer for 3 minutes, then remove from the heat.

Remove the tart from the oven and change the oven setting to medium to high grill (broil).

Pour the topping over the tart and brown under the grill, about 2–3 minutes, or until bubbly and dark brown. Watch it carefully to avoid burning.

Serve with cream.

Serves 12–16

Photo on page 152

I was born in Bulawayo, in what was then called Rhodesia. Our story is not unusual; as a four-year-old my dad fled Lithuania in 1938 with his family for South Africa, then moved again to southern Rhodesia, only to uproot again when the country was devastated by civil war. I remember packing our belongings and driving in convoy with armed guards into South Africa. Much later, newly married, I packed again and moved to Sydney.

I enjoy cooking simple family meals but my real passion is for baking. My grandmother spoilt us with bulkas, babkes and other sweet treats. Sadly, her recipes are long lost.

My mum, Ruth Eskin, gave me this recipe years and years ago. I make several of them every year during Pesach and also when I am entertaining friends who are gluten intolerant. It makes a lovely dessert, drizzled with melted chocolate and served with thick cream on the side. – Natanya Eskin

Date and chocolate torte

250 G (1½ CUPS) WHOLE ALMONDS

250 G (9 OZ) DARK CHOCOLATE, BROKEN INTO PIECES

6 EGG WHITES

115 G (4 OZ/½ CUP) CASTER (SUPERFINE) SUGAR

250 G (1½ CUPS) PITTED DATES, FINELY CHOPPED

250 ML (1 CUP) PURE CREAM (35% FAT), WHIPPED, FOR SERVING

TOPPING

180 G (6½ OZ) DARK CHOCOLATE, GRATED

Start this recipe the day before serving.

Preheat the oven to 180°C (350°F/Gas 4). Grease and line a 24 cm (9½ inch) springform cake tin.

Place the almonds and chocolate in the bowl of a food processor and chop into chunky pieces.

Whisk the egg whites until soft peaks form, then gradually add the sugar, whisking until thick and glossy. Fold in the almonds, chocolate and dates. Pour into the prepared tin and bake for 45 minutes. Turn off the oven and leave the torte inside to cool, with the door slightly open.

When the torte is cool, place on a platter and refrigerate overnight.

To make the topping, melt the chocolate in a heatproof bowl over a saucepan of simmering water. Do not allow the water to touch the bowl. Cool slightly and, using a spoon, drizzle over the cake.

Serve with a bowl of the whipped cream alongside.

Serves 10–12

Read Natanya's story on page 14

RUTH SADDICK

My love for food began at the age of three when I was old enough to understand the difference between the satay man's call and the ice-cream street cart's bell.

Born to Jewish Iraqi parents who called Singapore home for over 40 years, and growing up in an exotic place where food surrounded us like a rich dense cloak, I could not help but fall in love with food. Life in Singapore was a daily food adventure. It took me to the wet markets with Mum for fish, vegetables and exotic fruit, and to Little India with Dad, who left me to wander around the sacks of freshly ground cumin, coriander, cloves, cinnamon quills and saffron while he attended to his business. I touched and tasted everything, and still do.

My mum, daily and with complete serenity, transformed simple market ingredients into food that was exquisite in every sense. I was in constant awe of her beauty and culinary ability, and remain inspired by her mastery of Chinese, Malay, Indian, Nonya, Iraqi and Western traditions. She is behind my passion to keep this culinary style alive, and is my inspiration. What I have learned from Mum has taken years; I have been blessed with a master teacher. Now I do the same for my children and for theirs – it is the greatest gift I have to give them. And, of course, my love.

{Baclava}

Baclava

SYRUP

700 g (2 cups) **HONEY**

250 ml (1 cup) **WATER**

440 g (2 cups) **SUGAR**

100 ml **LEMON JUICE** (about 2 **lemons**)

2 tablespoons rosewater, orange blossom water or orange juice

This recipe needs to be started at least 5 hours ahead of serving.

Preheat the oven to 180°C (350°F/Gas 4). Butter a 20 cm (8 inch) square cake tin.

To make the syrup, place all the ingredients in a small saucepan and stir well. Bring to a rolling boil, then simmer, stirring often, for 30–40 minutes until the syrup coats the back of a metal spoon and has the consistency of light honey, or until a sugar thermometer placed in the syrup reaches 115°C (230°F). Set the syrup aside and bring it back to the boil when you are ready to take the baclava out of the oven.

To make the filling, chop the almonds to a medium consistency in a food processor. Place in a bowl and mix well with the sugar, cinnamon, cardamom and orange zest.

Unwrap the filo pastry, lay it out flat on the bench and cover with a damp tea towel (dish towel) to stop it drying out.

To roll the baclava, lay out one piece of filo horizontally. Keep the remaining filo covered. With a pastry brush, lightly brush the melted butter over the pastry, then top with another sheet of pastry. Continue until you have four pieces of filo laid out, brushing each layer with butter. Butter the top layer. If the butter cools too much, return to the heat briefly. Sprinkle ¾ cup of the filling on top, spreading it evenly out to the corners. Top the filling with another 2 layers of filo, buttering each one.

Fold in all four edges about 2 cm (¾ inch), creating a border to keep the nuts from falling out, then lightly brush the edges with butter. Starting with the edge closest to you, roll as tightly as possible into a sausage. Cut into 2 cm (¾ inch) wide rolls. Place each roll, cut sides facing upwards, in the buttered tin, packing them in tightly together. The rolls need to be well compacted. (Don't worry if the filling seems a bit loose when you are transferring the cut pieces to the tin. Once the syrup is poured over the baclava, the nuts will adhere to the filo.) Repeat with the remaining filling and filo, probably twice more.

For most Jewish families in Singapore, a tray of baclava and a bowl of seasoned fruit would complete the family Shabbat meal. My mother would make her own pastry, which was a lengthy and tedious procedure – there was no food processor or Mixmaster in those days. She would chop the almonds by hand and grind the spices at the time of baking; there was something special in the air at home when she baked these. This recipe is a modern version of my mother's. I can promise you, though, it tastes just as good!

FILLING
300 G (2 CUPS) WHOLE ALMONDS
55 G (¼ CUP) SUGAR
½ TEASPOON GROUND CINNAMON
½ TEASPOON GROUND
   CARDAMOM
FINELY GRATED ZEST OF 1
   ORANGE

1 PACKET (375 G/13¼ OZ)
   FILO PASTRY, AT ROOM
   TEMPERATURE FOR 2 HOURS
250 G (9 OZ) UNSALTED BUTTER,
   MELTED

When all the rolls are in the tin, drizzle a teaspoon of the remaining melted butter over each cut roll. Bake for 45 minutes, or until golden in colour.

In the meantime, check the syrup is still hot.

Remove the tin from the oven and immediately spoon the hot syrup over each roll. Set aside to absorb the syrup for at least 4 hours, or overnight. Do not refrigerate. Any left-over syrup can be drizzled on the serving platter.

To serve, remove the baclava from the tin. If this proves difficult, soften the syrup by sitting the tin in a sink of hot water.

Makes approximately 40 baclava

Photo on page 189

Fressing

Fressing is a word from Yiddish that has no literal translation. It is not just eating. It is eating purely for pleasure and with abandon; when you're not hungry, without looking at the time of day ... with just a little guilt. My family and many of my friends are fressers – how I truly love to feed them all, reaping joy and nachas *when they eat with gusto. Who can resist grabbing just one more meat blintz from the fridge?*

Lisa xx

Recipes

{Khachapuri}

Yoghurt is a commonly used ingredient in Persian cooking and this recipe was regularly served in my childhood home. One bowl is never enough! Serve this dip at room temperature with pita bread, salad or on top of rice.

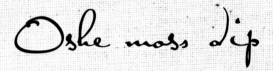

½ BUNCH SILVERBEET (SWISS
   CHARD), THICK STALKS
   REMOVED, TO YIELD 200 G (7 OZ)
80 ML (⅓ CUP) OLIVE OIL
3 ONIONS, SLICED LENGTHWAYS
   ALONG THE GRAIN
SEA SALT AND FRESHLY GROUND
   BLACK PEPPER
520 G (1 LB 2 ½ OZ/2 CUPS)
   UNSWEETENED GREEK-STYLE
   YOGHURT
1–2 CLOVES GARLIC, CRUSHED,
   OR TO TASTE
1 X 400 G (14 OZ) TIN CANNELLINI
   BEANS, RINSED AND DRAINED

Wash and chop the silverbeet. Place in a saucepan, cover and steam, with no extra water, until completely wilted, a few minutes. Set aside to cool.

Heat the oil in a small frying pan and fry the onion over medium heat until well caramelised and a deep golden brown, about 20 minutes. Add salt to taste and set aside to cool.

Mix the silverbeet with the yoghurt, salt, pepper, garlic and beans. Once the onion has cooled, spoon, together with any remaining cooking oil, on top of the dip.

Makes 4 cups

My darling mum, Jeannette, lived a prosperous and sheltered early life in Tehran, Iran (Persia), with a close family who were merchants along the trade route to Palestine. In 1952, her father moved the Cadry clan to Australia.

Cooking has always been a central feature in our lives. Omi, mum's mother, could quickly throw together an exotic dinner and guests would come from near and far to share her food, which was so full of flavour and life. She never had written recipes – they were all passed down to her, and then to my mother, by sight, smell and taste.

When I married, Mum and Omi would stand for hours, week after week, teaching me their many Persian dishes. I would stand with pen and paper and meticulously write down every single thing. They would often simply say, 'just keep adding till it tastes right'.

I miss those days of being in the kitchen with three generations connected by love, laughter and food. Mum was only 53 when she passed away, leaving behind a legacy started by Omi of a loving family that gathers, in good times and bad, around the large dining room table surrounded by lots of great food. (See also Nikki's poppy seed cake on page 229.)

MAISIE WINKLER

The women of Maisie's Sephardic Iraqi family loved to cook. Recipes were neither precise nor written down; rather, they were lovingly passed down so that every young bride's culinary trousseau included instructions on how to cook family favourites for their new husbands.

Born in Singapore in 1929, Maisie, together with all the women of the family, was evacuated to Bombay during the war and eventually Australia where she met and married Andre Winkler. He yearned for the Ashkenazi Hungarian dishes of his own childhood, yet in Maisie he found a new world of Middle Eastern Jewish cooking.

As a Chazzan's wife, Maisie entertained often and authentic Sephardic cooking always comprised part of the menu. Her dinner parties in their little Lindfield home were legendary, introducing Australian Jews to new tastes and flavours. As an observant family, they did not eat out of the home, so Maisie, often with Andre's help, cooked nearly every day, always trying to create something innovative and wonderful.

Though battling serious illness for nearly a decade, Maisie never lost the will to prepare and serve beautiful food for her family and friends. Her passing in 1979 left, among so much else, a culinary void that was never filled, particularly for Andre. Yet Maisie's daughters, Charmaine and Janine, continue to cook Sephardic recipes for their families from those passed down through the women of their family and which Maisie, in beautiful British-school cursive, finally wrote down in her recipe books. With five daughters between them, they hope the recipes will continue to delight generations to come.

These vegetable puffs were originally served on Shavuot when it is customary not to eat meat. The preparation took place with military precision, and as assistants, Charmaine and Janine used to help roll the dough, cut out the circles, and spoon in the filling. The final step was the domain of the head chef, as Maisie braided the edges and sealed the puff with a fork.

Maisie's samboosacs

OIL PASTRY
450 G (1 LB/3 CUPS) SELF-RAISING
   FLOUR
½ TEASPOON SALT
185 ML (¾ CUP) VEGETABLE OIL
125 ML (½ CUP) COLD WATER

FILLING
2 ONIONS, FINELY SLICED
2 TABLESPOONS VEGETABLE OIL
1 CELERY STALK, FINELY SLICED
1 CLOVE GARLIC, CRUSHED
100 G (3½ OZ) MINCED (GROUND)
   BEEF (OPTIONAL)
2 TEASPOONS CURRY POWDER OR
   1 TEASPOON MADRAS CURRY
   PASTE
PINCH OF DRIED CHILLI FLAKES
2 TEASPOONS LEMON JUICE, OR
   TO TASTE
SEA SALT
2 POTATOES, BOILED AND
   MASHED (200 G/7 OZ OF MASH)
40 G (¼ CUP) PEAS, BLANCHED

To make the pastry, process all the ingredients in a food processor until a ball of dough forms. Wrap in plastic wrap and rest in the fridge for 1 hour while you make the filling.

In a large frying pan over medium–high heat, cook the onion in the oil until soft and golden, about 15 minutes. Add the celery and garlic and cook for a further 10 minutes. Add the beef, if using, and continue to cook until browned all over. Stir in the curry powder or paste and cook for a few minutes until aromatic. Add the chilli flakes, lemon juice and salt to taste, and then add the potato and peas. Cook together for 2 minutes to combine the flavours. Allow to cool for 15 minutes.

Preheat the oven to 180°C (350°F/Gas 4). Line a baking tray.

Divide the pastry into four equal portions and roll out each ball between 2 sheets of baking paper until 2–3 mm (¹⁄₁₆–⅛ inch) thick, and then refrigerate each piece until needed. Cut out circles with a 9 cm (3½ inch) cookie cutter or glass. Place 1 teaspoon of filling in the centre of each circle. Lightly moisten the edge of one-half of the circle, then gather up the opposite half to create a semicircle, enclosing all the filling. Press the edges together with your fingers. Either crimp the edge and allow to remain upright or place the samboosac flat on the prepared tray and press down with a fork to seal the edge. Repeat until all the pastry circles and filling have been used. Bake for 30 minutes, or until golden.

Makes approximately 24 samboosacs

Photo on page 200

{Maisie's samboosacs}

{Russian blintzes}

LENA TOROPOVA

All Russian women make blintzes – rolled and filled crepes which are then lightly fried to serve. At our deli we cook them exactly how my mum and friend Lora have always done, with a perfect soft texture that can be filled and rolled easily. We can make 500 in an average week, and many more at festivals like Shavuot. The blintzes can be cooked, rolled and refrigerated and then reheated and served several days later.

Russian blintzes

BEEF FILLING

2 KG (4 LB 8 OZ) BEEF BLADE,
    BRISKET AND/OR TOP RIB
2 LARGE ONIONS, SLICED ALONG
    THE GRAIN
60 ML (¼ CUP) VEGETABLE OIL
SEA SALT AND FRESHLY GROUND
    BLACK PEPPER

**EGG AND MUSHROOM
    FILLING**

1 SMALL ONION, SLICED ALONG
    THE GRAIN
2 TABLESPOONS VEGETABLE OIL
600 G (1 LB 5 OZ) BUTTON
    MUSHROOMS
2 EGGS, BOILED UNTIL JUST HARD

Make the filling well before rolling the blintzes, preferably the day before.

To make the beef filling, bring water to the boil in a large stockpot. Add the meat and simmer for 1½–2 hours, or until fork tender. Allow the meat to cool in the cooking liquid. When cool, remove the meat and reserve the liquid. In a frying pan over high heat, fry the onion in the oil until soft and golden. Strain the onion to remove the cooking oil. Mince the meat and onion together and season generously with salt and pepper. Moisten with a few spoonfuls of the reserved cooking liquid so the meat mixture is not dry.

To make the egg and mushroom filling, fry the onion in the oil in a frying pan over low–medium heat until golden, about 20 minutes. Add the mushrooms and cook for 30 minutes until the flavours are well combined, the mushrooms are soft and there is no liquid in the pan. Process the eggs in a food processor until crumbly. Remove and set aside. Process the cooked mushrooms in a food processor until chunky. In a bowl, combine the mushrooms and eggs and season generously with salt and pepper. Allow to cool.

To make the crepe batter, mix together the flour, sugar and salt in a bowl. Make a well in the centre and pour in the milk or water. Starting in the centre, slowly incorporate all the flour into the liquid with a wooden spoon. Stir in the eggs and strain the mixture into a clean bowl. Add the oil and mix gently. The mixture should be like runny cream. Add more liquid if needed. Cook the mixture immediately, without allowing the batter to sit for too long.

CREPE BATTER

300 G (10½ OZ/2 CUPS) PLAIN (ALL-
  PURPOSE) FLOUR
2 TEASPOONS SUGAR
LARGE PINCH OF SALT
500 ML (2 CUPS) MILK OR WATER
3 EGGS, LIGHTLY WHISKED
1 TABLESPOON VEGETABLE OIL (IF
  USING WATER, ADD AN EXTRA 2
  TEASPOONS OIL)

LIGHT OLIVE OIL, FOR FRYING
VEGETABLE OIL, FOR FRYING

Brush a 22–23 cm (8½–9 inch) crepe pan with a little light olive oil. Heat the pan over medium heat. Put a ladleful of batter in the pan and swirl so it spreads easily to the edge of the pan. If it doesn't spread easily, add a little more liquid to the batter. Over medium–high heat, cook the crepe for about 30 seconds on one side only and when the mixture has firmed and is lightly browned underneath, flip over onto a baking paper-lined chopping board, cooked side facing up. Put each crepe on top of the next.

When all the crepes are cooked, put two layers of paper towel on top of the stack. Place the chopping board on a wire rack, and then cover with a cake dome or large bowl for 5–10 minutes.

To roll the blintzes, place a large spoon of filling (about 40 g/1½ oz) across the middle of the crepe on the cooked side. Fold the edge of the crepe over the meat and tuck in underneath. Tighten by pulling the log towards you and continue to roll to just over halfway. Fold the sides in, tucking in a little so that the unrolled edges are parallel. Continue to roll up, tightening the log once along the way. Place the blintzes seam side down on a plate. The uncooked side will now be the outside of the blintz.

To serve, gently fry the blintzes in a little vegetable oil until light golden brown and place in a heatproof dish. When ready to serve, heat uncovered in a hot oven or microwave.

Makes 20 blintzes

NOTE: If you keep kosher, use water rather than the milk when making meat blintzes. The original recipe for the mushroom blintzes uses canned sliced champignons because Lena finds it better for the vast quantities they make in the deli. For the home cook, button mushrooms work well.

Photo on page 201
Read Lena's story on page 249

ALICE ZASLAVSKY

My family moved to Georgia at the turn of the century to escape the pogroms in Russia and the Ukraine. My parents decided to immigrate to Australia when the country was on the brink of civil war, and we settled in Sydney in 1991. The Jewish community was very supportive on our arrival; in fact, we still have the Kiddush cup that was given to us as a welcome gesture. My parents' initial plan was to set up a Georgian restaurant, but, with no hospitality experience and two PhDs between them, they were advised to stick to what they knew. Not long after, we moved to Melbourne.

Being Jewish and Georgian, food was always going to be a big part of my life. I learned to cook by watching and helping Mum and Dad in the kitchen, especially at times when they were preparing feasts for guests – something that happened almost on a weekly basis (and still does). My job was to flip eggplants, peel potatoes and set the table. Funnily enough, they're still the only jobs Dad will let me do.

My strongest food memories still come from my childhood. I fondly remember sitting in the garden of my grandfather's dacha *(weekend home) gorging myself on figs, persimmons and plums picked straight from the trees, while Grandpa wasn't looking. I'd help my grandmother make her special meat dumplings and, when tomatoes were ripe and abundant, the whole family pitched in to make* satsebeli, *a spiced Georgian tomato sauce. We weren't a foodie family – we were, and are, simply a family that loves food.*

Every Georgian woman makes her own version of khachapuri and it graces the tables of most family celebrations. My mum, Professor Frada Burstein, took a cheese pie to her very first staff party when she joined Monash University. The head of school said if she continued to feed them like that, she would always have a job there. This is her recipe.

Khachapuri

PASTRY

225 G (8 oz/1½ cups) **PLAIN**
   (ALL-PURPOSE) **FLOUR**
½ TEASPOON SALT
30 ML (1½ tablespoons) **WHITE**
   VINEGAR
1 HEAPED TEASPOON
   BICARBONATE OF SODA (BAKING
   SODA)
150 G (5½ oz) **UNSWEETENED**
   GREEK-STYLE YOGHURT
25 ML (1 TABLESPOON PLUS 1 TEASPOON)
   OLIVE OIL

FILLING

1 EGG
200 G (7 oz) **CREAMED COTTAGE**
   CHEESE
100 G (3½ oz) **FETA CHEESE**
100 G (3½ oz) **GRATED**
   MOZZARELLA CHEESE
SEA SALT AND FRESHLY GROUND
   BLACK PEPPER

OLIVE OIL, FOR FRYING AND
   DRIZZLING
KNOB OF BUTTER, FOR SERVING

To make the pastry, mix the flour and salt together in a bowl. Make a well in the centre. Add the vinegar and then the bicarbonate of soda. Allow it to bubble. Add the yoghurt and oil and mix together in the well. Bring in the flour, then knead for 5 minutes until you have a smooth elastic dough (add more flour if needed). Rest the dough for 30 minutes or so.

To make the filling, combine all the ingredients and mash together with a fork or stick blender. Season to taste.

Divide the dough into 4 balls. Take one ball and divide into two. Roll each half into a thin circle, about 20 cm (8 inches) in diameter, with one circle slightly bigger. Spread 2 dessertspoons of filling across the bigger circle and top with the smaller circle. Bring the edge over to seal and pat down to flatten the pie.

Heat 1 teaspoon of the olive oil in a frying pan over low–medium heat and gently fry the pie face down until golden brown. Drizzle a little olive oil over the top side before turning it over and frying on the other side until golden. Top with a knob of butter while still hot, before serving.

Repeat with the remaining dough balls and filling.

Serve hot.

Makes 4 individual or 2 larger pies

Photo on page 194

Mum created this recipe sometime in the 1970s, and from then on she took it to everyone's house for Shabbat dinner, whether she was asked to or not! It became her own little tradition and is still remembered fondly. She taught my daughter Eliza this recipe over many visits to Sydney, and now Eliza makes it to the exact taste of her grandmother's. – Merelyn Chalmers

Avocado dip

½ WHITE ONION

2 TABLESPOONS BUTTER, AT
   ROOM TEMPERATURE

PINCH OF CAYENNE PEPPER

SEA SALT AND FRESHLY GROUND
   BLACK PEPPER

4 EGGS, HARD BOILED AND
   PEELED

2 LARGE RIPE AVOCADOS

2 TABLESPOONS LEMON JUICE, OR
   TO TASTE

Chop the onion as finely as possible (do not grate as it becomes bitter). Place in a bowl and mix with the butter, cayenne pepper and a generous pinch of salt and pepper until combined.

Grate the eggs directly on top of the onion mix. Peel and deseed the avocados, grate directly on top of the eggs, then mix well with a fork. (Grating the avocado and egg gives the dip a different texture to using a food processor or mashing.) Add the lemon juice, stir well, taste and adjust seasoning as required. You should be able to taste the tang of lemon and the kick of cayenne.

Transfer to a serving bowl, cover tightly with foil (keeping out the light helps maintain the green colour) and refrigerate for at least 1 hour before serving. Serve with challah or crackers.

Serves 10

Read Merelyn's story on page 14

This Dutch cake is one of my childhood favourites, a recipe from the marvellous Charmaine Solomon. It is a rich, sweet, yeasted sultana bread traditionally served with Dutch edam cheese and unsalted butter. To this day it takes me back to my childhood – I used to get so excited when I would see the ruby red wax covering of the cheese, as I knew I was in for a treat. It is also delicious toasted.

DOUGH
125 ML (½ CUP) MILK
3 TEASPOONS CASTER (SUPERFINE)
** SUGAR**
2 TEASPOONS SEA SALT
90 G (3¼ OZ) BUTTER
375 ML (1½ CUPS) WARM WATER
30 G (1 OZ) FRESH YEAST OR
1½ SACHETS (10 G/3 TEASPOONS)
** DRIED ACTIVE YEAST**
825–900 G (1 LB 13 OZ–2 LB/
** 5½–6 CUPS) BREAD FLOUR, SIFTED**

BREUDHER
315 G (11 OZ) UNSALTED BUTTER,
** AT ROOM TEMPERATURE**
315 G (11 OZ/1⅓ CUPS) CASTER
** (SUPERFINE) SUGAR**
5 EGGS
2 TEASPOONS VANILLA EXTRACT
240 G (1½ CUPS) SULTANAS
** (GOLDEN RAISINS)**

Heat the milk in a saucepan until just boiling, then stir in the sugar, salt and butter. Allow to cool to lukewarm. Pour the warm water into a large bowl and add the yeast, stirring until dissolved. Add the lukewarm milk mixture. Add 3 cups of the flour to the bowl. Combine gently with a wooden spoon until smooth, then add more of the flour to make a soft dough. Turn onto a lightly floured board and knead for a few minutes until just smooth and elastic. Shape into a smooth ball and place in an oiled bowl, turning the dough over to oil the top. Cover with a clean cloth and leave in a warm place to rise until doubled in bulk, about 1 hour.

Grease two 2.5 litre (10 cup) bundt or kugelhopf tins. When the dough has risen, cream the butter and sugar in an electric mixer until pale and creamy. Add the dough in small pieces, beating well, until all the dough has been incorporated. Add the eggs, one at a time, beating well after each addition. Stir in the vanilla and sultanas until well combined. Divide the dough between the two tins and leave in a warm place to rise for 30 minutes, or until almost doubled in size.

Meanwhile, preheat the oven to 160°C (315°F).

Bake the breudher for 30–35 minutes, or until well risen and golden brown on top and a skewer comes out clean when inserted into the centre. If the top starts to brown too quickly, cover with foil. Cool in the tins for 10 minutes, then turn onto a wire rack to cool completely.

Serve the breudher sliced and spread with unsalted butter and thin slices of edam cheese.

Makes 2 cakes
Each cake serves 10–12

Photo on page 206

PATRICIA LILING

Growing up in exotic Sri Lanka at a decadent time, my parents were either always hosting a lavish party or on their way to one. The food was spectacular, whether a tasty morsel of finger food or the banquet that followed. In 1973, as a young girl, I left Colombo with my family for Australia, moving around quite a bit and eventually settling in Sydney in the mid 1980s.

Our home was always full of good food and many people. As a new immigrant growing up in the suburbs, I would go to school with weird and wonderful things in my lunchbox when all I wanted was a Vegemite sandwich and a Milk Arrowroot biscuit.

My mother ruled the kitchen, easily able to replicate whatever she ate outside the home. She was a hard act to follow, and my first nervous attempts at cooking were during my days of shared student housing. After I married, I suddenly paid attention to my mother's cooking and slowly mastered a variety of traditional and non-traditional foods.

Having married an Israeli whose parents had European backgrounds, a typical week in my house could see me cooking anything from chicken soup, curry with fragrant rice to brownies and spaghetti bolognese. The best part about this is that my three children have grown up with developed and adventurous palates, experiencing the best of two very different cultures through food. Our memories of places travelled always seem to be 'what delicious thing we ate' and then the joy of later recreating it at home.

SHEREEN AARON

Food is such a huge part of my life – it's creative, inspiring, nourishing and satisfying. My cooking is a mix of Ashkenazi and Sephardi. We routinely have a typical Ashkenazi Shabbat dinner; challah, chicken soup and roast chicken. Then on Sunday night we share dinner with my husband Allan's Sephardi family; spicy stews or curries, shorba *(chicken rice soup),* hushua *(stuffed chicken), yellow rice and fried eggplant.*

However, my real passion is baking. Preparing, kneading and shaping pastries and breads really connects me with the food I am creating. It is such a joy to pull a kugelhopf from the oven and watch the delight on my friends' and family's faces.

My strongest food influences are my grandmother Nanna Cooch from Romania (named because she would always pinch cheeks and say 'coochie coo') and my mother, Ziggy, who is legendary for her entertaining and repertoire of cakes. My own home centres around the kitchen. I love a challenge and often experiment and try to replicate dishes my family have seen on TV or eaten in restaurants. Friends and family are welcomed by the aromas of cakes, pastries and breads, along with flavoursome curries and sauces. (See also Shereen's yellow rice on page 163.)

I have always loved an authentic boiled bagel but it is not always easy to find. The solution? Make your own. These have become a quick and easy snack at my place.

Boiled bagels

2 SACHETS (14 G/1 TABLESPOON)
   DRIED YEAST
375 ML (1½ CUPS) WARM WATER
3 TABLESPOONS CASTER
   (SUPERFINE) SUGAR
565 G (1 LB 4½ OZ/3¾ CUPS) BREAD
   FLOUR, PLUS EXTRA ½ CUP, FOR
   KNEADING
1 TABLESPOON SALT
1 TABLESPOON SUGAR
SESAME OR POPPY SEEDS, FOR
   SPRINKLING (OPTIONAL)
SEA SALT, FOR SPRINKLING
   (OPTIONAL)

In a small bowl, mix the yeast with the warm water and 1 teaspoon of the caster sugar. Allow to stand for 10 minutes, or until it froths.

In a large bowl, combine the flour with the remaining caster sugar and the salt. Make a well in the centre and pour in the yeast mixture. Working the flour in from the sides, slowly incorporate together. Once a soft dough forms, turn out onto a lightly floured surface. Knead and stretch the dough with your hands until it is smooth and elastic, about 8–10 minutes. You can do this with a dough hook in an electric mixer if you prefer. If the dough becomes too sticky, add some of the extra flour. Place the dough in an oiled bowl. Cover with plastic wrap and then a tea towel (dish towel). Allow to rise in a warm place for 15–20 minutes.

When the dough has risen, tip it onto a bench and cut into 12 equal portions. Without working the dough too much, shape each piece into a smooth ball by stretching the dough over itself and tucking it in underneath. Poke a hole in the centre with your thumb, and gently enlarge the hole while working the bagel into a uniform shape. Ensure you make the hole large enough so that when the dough rises again you can still see the hole.

Place the bagels well apart on a tray and cover with baking paper and a cloth. Allow to rise for 20 minutes. If they rise for too long, the bagels will shrivel when boiled.

Preheat the oven to 190°C (375°F/Gas 5). Line a large baking tray.

Fill a wide deep frying pan with water. Bring to the boil, add the sugar, stirring to dissolve. When the bagels have finished their second rise, slip them into the water, four or so at a time, smooth side down. Cook for 2 minutes on each side. Remove carefully from the water with two forks and place on the prepared tray, smooth side up. Sprinkle immediately with your choice of seeds or sea salt. Bake for 25–35 minutes, or until golden brown.

Makes 12 bagels

While living in the US, my family craved the chocolate yeast kugelhopf we had left behind in Bondi. They nagged me until I created a recipe that tasted just as good and cured their nostalgia.

Chocolate yeast kugelhopf

185 ML (¾ CUP) MILK

1 SACHET (7 G/2¼ TEASPOONS) ACTIVE DRIED YEAST

80 G (2¾ OZ/⅓ CUP) CASTER (SUPERFINE) SUGAR, PLUS EXTRA, FOR SPRINKLING

450 G (1 LB/3 CUPS) BREAD FLOUR, PLUS EXTRA, FOR KNEADING

½ TEASPOON SALT

115 G (4 OZ) BUTTER

3 EGGS

1 TEASPOON VANILLA EXTRACT

1 EGG, LIGHTLY BEATEN, FOR EGG WASH

You will need a large angel (chiffon) cake tin with a removable base. Carefully line the side, base and funnel with baking paper.

Gently warm ¼ cup of the milk. Sprinkle with the yeast and 1 teaspoon of the sugar. Allow to stand for 5 minutes to allow it to froth. Add 3 teaspoons of the flour and stir. Allow to stand for 15–20 minutes, or until frothy and thick.

Mix the remaining flour and sugar together with the salt in the bowl of an electric mixer.

Warm the remaining milk and melt the butter.

Beat the eggs with the vanilla. Add these and the yeast mixture to the flour mixture and knead with the dough hook for 10 minutes. You may need to add extra flour but do so a spoon at a time, kneading after each addition. You will have a very sticky dough that just comes away from the side of the bowl.

Put the dough into an oiled bowl, cover with plastic wrap and a tea towel (dish towel). Put the bowl in a warm place and allow to rise until doubled in size. This will take at least 2 hours.

Once the dough has risen, make the filling. Place the filling ingredients in a large heatproof bowl over a saucepan of simmering water (or use a double boiler) and melt, stirring until smooth.

FILLING

300 G (10½ OZ) BEST-QUALITY DARK
    CHOCOLATE, CHOPPED
60 G (2¼ OZ) BUTTER
115 G (½ CUP) CASTER (SUPERFINE)
    SUGAR
25 G (¼ CUP) COCOA POWDER
½ TEASPOON GROUND CINNAMON

Cut the dough in half. Roll out to form a large rectangle (30 x 45 cm/12 x 17¾ inches) and carefully spread half the filling mixture on the surface from edge to edge. Roll up the dough to make a large snake and place it into the prepared tin, curling around the funnel, seam side up. Repeat with the other half of the dough. Place it on top of the first roll, seam side down. Cover with plastic wrap and a tea towel and allow to rise in a warm place until at least doubled in size, about 1 hour. It will rise almost to the edge of the tin. Brush gently with the egg wash and sprinkle with the extra sugar.

Preheat the oven to 170°C (325°F/Gas 3).

Bake the kugelhopf for 40 minutes, or until well risen and golden brown on top. If not eating immediately, allow to cool out of the tin but with the baking paper still attached.

Best eaten on the day of baking or reheated the next day. Freezes well for up to 3 months.

Serves 10–12

Photo on page 216

{Chocolate yeast kugelhopf}

{Caramel torte}

My grandmother was a typical doting Yiddishe nanna, and this was one of her most memorable cakes, all of which (as she always said) had to have ta'am (the right taste). This recipe was a closely guarded secret but the time has now come to share it with the world. The caramel recipe can be doubled for a more luscious effect.

Caramel torte

340 G (11¾ OZ/2¼ CUPS) PLAIN (ALL-PURPOSE) FLOUR

2 TABLESPOONS CASTER (SUPERFINE) SUGAR

115 G (4 OZ) UNSALTED BUTTER, AT ROOM TEMPERATURE

125 ML (½ CUP) PURE CREAM (35% FAT)

1 EGG, LIGHTLY BEATEN

40 G (¼ CUP) TOASTED OR SUGARED ALMONDS, FOR GARNISH

This recipe is best made the day before serving.

Preheat the oven to 170°C (325°F/Gas 3). Line three or four large baking trays.

Put the flour and sugar into a large bowl. Using your fingertips, rub in the butter until it resembles coarse crumbs. In a separate bowl, whip the cream until slightly thickened and stir in the egg. Add this to the flour mixture and combine until it just comes together as a dough.

Divide the dough into 9 pieces. On a lightly floured surface roll out, one piece at a time, to a thickness of 1–2 mm (⅟₃₂–⅟₁₆ inch). Using a 24 cm (9½ inch) circle as a guide (the base of a springform cake tin works well) cut a circle from the dough. Lift carefully and place on a prepared tray. Continue until 9 circles have been rolled, cut out and placed on the trays. Place in the oven and bake until golden brown, about 20–30 minutes. Check regularly as different shelves of the oven may cook at different temperatures.

To make the caramel sauce, melt the sugar in a saucepan over medium heat until all the grains are dissolved and it is a golden brown caramel. Do not stir or move it around, and watch it carefully. Warm the milk a little, stir in the bicarbonate of soda, then slowly pour the milk into the caramel a little at a time, stirring constantly. Don't worry if the mixture seizes, it will melt again. Bring to the boil over low heat until slightly thickened. Add the butter and vanilla and stir until combined and thick. Remove from the heat and allow to cool slightly until thick enough to spoon onto

CARAMEL SAUCE

295 G (10¼ OZ/1⅓ CUPS) SUGAR

200 ML (¾ CUP PLUS 1 TABLESPOON) MILK

¼ TEASPOON BICARBONATE OF SODA (BAKING SODA)

125 G (4½ OZ) BUTTER

½ TEASPOON VANILLA EXTRACT

the pastry layers.

To assemble, place a drop of the sauce on a cake plate and cover with the first disc of pastry. Spoon 2 dessertspoons of caramel over the disc and spread thinly from edge to edge. Top with the next disc and a layer of caramel and continue until all the discs and caramel are used, making sure you keep enough caramel for the top. Spread the remaining caramel over the top disc and garnish with the nuts. Leave the torte to sit, covered, at least overnight before serving.

Serves 10

Photo on page 217

SUE SANDER

I am one of a rare breed of the Perth Jewish community, as I was born and bred here. I remember enormous family celebrations in our backyard when I was young. The 44 gallon drum barbecue was fired up with a zillion chops and sausages. There were enormous bowls of salads and the hugest watermelons halved and hollowed out for dessert.

My mum, originally from London, cooked traditional simple food to feed a large hungry family. As a young girl I loved going with my dad, a Mediterranean cook, to the Greek and Italian stores where I'd sit on top of the olive tins, eating morsels of unusual but delicious food.

My deep passion for food began when I became a vegetarian 30 years ago. My late brother, with his Magic Apple Wholefood restaurants, was way ahead of his time in whole foods and vegetarian cooking. He always said 'we are what we eat' and I have lived by that motto ever since. I always enjoyed looking in on my young children when fast asleep, knowing that I had filled their bellies with healthy food on which to grow and develop. Through their teen years, our children's friends always knew their favourite biscuits, slices and muffins would be in one of the many tins on top of or in the fridge. Mama Sue's biscuit tins had their own reputation!

I found this recipe while working with a lady who is gluten intolerant. At that time there weren't many recipes for her dietary needs and I wanted to make a special cake for her birthday. It's quite large, always popular and well suited for dessert. It's also great for Passover – a bonus!

Flourless apple, almond and ginger cake

3 GRANNY SMITH APPLES

30 G (1 oz) UNSALTED BUTTER

50 G (1¾ oz/¼ CUP) CASTER
  (SUPERFINE) SUGAR

2 WHOLE CLOVES

80 G (½ CUP) RAISINS

260 G (9¼ oz/2⅓ CUPS) GROUND
  ALMONDS

220 G (1½ CUPS) WHOLE ALMONDS

2½ TEASPOONS GROUND GINGER

2 TEASPOONS BAKING POWDER

4 EGGS

230 G (8½ oz/1 CUP) RAW
  (DEMERARA) SUGAR

145 ML (½ CUP PLUS 1 TABLESPOON)
  PURE MAPLE OR GOLDEN SYRUP
  (LIGHT TREACLE)

TOPPING

2 ROYAL GALA OR GOLDEN
  DELICIOUS APPLES

50 G (⅓ CUP) WHOLE ALMONDS,
  COARSELY CHOPPED

50 G (1¾ oz) BUTTER, MELTED

50 G (¼ CUP) RAW (DEMERARA) SUGAR

Preheat the oven to 180°C (350°F/Gas 4). Grease and line a 26 cm (10½ inch) springform cake tin.

Peel and core the apples, then cut into wedges.

Over medium heat, melt the butter in a frying pan large enough to fit the apples in one layer. Add the apple wedges, caster sugar and cloves and toss to combine. Cook, stirring occasionally, until the apples are well coated, soft and starting to colour, about 5–10 minutes. There should be no liquid left in the pan. Remove the cloves, add the raisins and cook for another minute or so to soften. Remove from the heat and cool.

Process the ground almonds, whole almonds, ginger and baking powder in a food processor until coarsely chopped. Set aside.

In an electric mixer, whisk the eggs, raw sugar and maple or golden syrup until light and fluffy. Fold in the nut mixture and cooked apples. Pour into the prepared tin.

To make the topping, core and thinly slice the apples and arrange over the cake batter, overlapping slightly. Scatter the almonds on top, pour the melted butter over and then sprinkle on the sugar.

Bake the cake for about 1–1¼ hours until golden and cooked through and a skewer inserted in the middle comes out clean. If the cake is browning too quickly, cover with some foil.

Cool completely in the tin and serve at room temperature with plain yoghurt or vanilla ice cream.

Serves 12–16

An apple pie was made by Mum virtually every Friday, ready to serve when people dropped in for afternoon tea on Saturday. She often served it with whipped cream laced with cognac. Over the years she took short cuts – a dairy-free-push-in-the-tin pastry, a quick open of a tin of pie apple – but this is her original recipe, and by far the best. The apples can be made and refrigerated the day before assembling the pie. – Merelyn Chalmers

Yolan's apple pie

STEWED APPLES

1.2 KG (2 LB 12 OZ) GRANNY SMITH
  APPLES, ABOUT 8 MEDIUM
60 G (2¼ OZ) UNSALTED BUTTER
2 TABLESPOONS SUGAR
¼ TEASPOON GROUND CINNAMON
¼ TEASPOON VANILLA EXTRACT

PASTRY

170 G (6 OZ) PLAIN (ALL-PURPOSE)
  FLOUR
115 G (4 OZ) COLD UNSALTED
  BUTTER
1 EGG YOLK
2 TABLESPOONS PURE CREAM
  (35% FAT)

To make the stewed apples, peel and core the apples and cut into thick slices. Melt the butter in a deep frying pan and add the sugar. Stir until melted and slightly browned. Add the apples to the butter mix and toss gently to combine. Place a lid on the pan, turn the heat to low and steam the apples for 10 minutes, or until tender. Remove the lid and add the cinnamon and vanilla. Continue to cook, uncovered, for a further 5 minutes, or until the liquid has reduced and the apples are almost dry. Do not over stir the apples, you don't want them to break up too much. Set aside to cool.

To make the pastry, place the flour in a bowl and grate the butter on top. Occasionally dip the butter into the flour to make it easier to grate. Rub the butter into the flour with your fingertips or a pastry cutter until it resembles coarse crumbs. Combine the egg yolk and cream, then pour onto the flour and mix by hand until a rough dough forms. Knead lightly on a lightly floured board, cover with plastic wrap and place in the fridge to rest for 1 hour.

Preheat the oven to 180°C (350°F/Gas 4). Butter and flour a 23 cm (9 inch) pie dish.

To assemble the pie, cut the pastry in half and reserve half for the top. On a lightly floured board, roll out the half to about 2–3 mm (1/16–1/8 inch) thick or large enough to fit the pie dish. Gently place the pastry into the prepared dish, leaving an overhang.

FILLING

55 G (½ CUP) GROUND ALMONDS

60 G (SCANT 1/3 CUP) CASTER
  (SUPERFINE) SUGAR

2 TABLESPOONS STRAWBERRY JAM

1 EGG WHITE

1 EGG, LIGHTLY BEATEN, FOR
  GLAZING

1 TABLESPOON SUGAR, FOR
  SPRINKLING

To make the filling, mix the ground almonds with the sugar. Spread the pastry base with the strawberry jam and sprinkle half the almond mixture on top. Whisk the egg white until stiff and gently fold into the cooked apple. Spoon the apple mix into the pastry base and sprinkle the remaining almond mix on top.

Roll out the other half of the pastry and place on top of the filling. Cut a small hole in the middle with a sharp knife to allow steam to escape. Press the edges of the pastry (top and bottom) together to seal, then trim the pastry to fit the dish. Press around the edge with a fork to decorate. If you like, cut leaf shapes out of any left-over pastry and place them on top.

Brush with the egg wash and sprinkle with the sugar. Bake for 45 minutes, or until golden.

Serves 8–10

Photos on page 225–6
Read Merelyn's story on page 14

{Yolan's apple pie}

Every week we have a cake on the Shabbat table and I love that our children come home to the welcoming smell of baking each and every Friday afternoon. My husband, Gary, is of Hungarian heritage and we are always in search of poppy seed recipes. Years ago I was given a basic cake recipe and over time it has evolved into this wonderful one, now the cake of choice for Gary's birthday.

Poppy seed cake

250 ML (1 CUP) MILK

135 G (1½ CUPS) GROUND POPPY
  SEEDS

200 G (7 oz) UNSALTED BUTTER, AT
  ROOM TEMPERATURE

345 G (12 oz/1½ CUPS) CASTER
  (SUPERFINE) SUGAR

FINELY GRATED ZEST OF 1
  ORANGE OR LEMON

3 EGGS

225 G (8 oz/1½ CUPS) SELF-RAISING
  FLOUR

GLAZE (OPTIONAL)

115 G (½ CUP) CASTER (SUPERFINE)
  SUGAR

JUICE OF 2 ORANGES AND 1
  LEMON

Preheat the oven to 170°C (325°F/Gas 3). Grease and line a 22 cm (8½ inch) springform cake tin.

Pour the milk into a saucepan and bring to boiling point. Add the poppy seeds, remove from the heat and leave to soften for 10 minutes.

In an electric mixer, beat the butter, sugar and zest until pale and creamy. Add the eggs one at a time, beating well after each addition. Mix in the poppy seed mixture and flour until just combined.

Pour into the prepared tin and bake for 50 minutes, or until a skewer inserted in the middle comes out clean.

To make the glaze, heat the sugar and the juice in a saucepan and stir over medium heat until the sugar is melted. Bring to the boil, then simmer until it is reduced by half and has a glaze consistency.

Pour the glaze over the warm cake. Allow to cool before removing from the tin to serve.

Serves 10–12

Read Nikki's story on page 196

Leah started baking for Sydney cafés and delis when her children had grown up, well before people were making homemade cakes for such places. This orange syrup cake was one of her most requested cakes. It is perfect with a dollop of whipped cream for afternoon tea or as a dessert.

Orange Syrup cake

250 G (9 OZ) UNSALTED BUTTER, AT
   ROOM TEMPERATURE
230 G (8½ OZ/1 CUP) CASTER
   (SUPERFINE) SUGAR
3 EGGS, SEPARATED
250 G (10½ OZ) SOUR CREAM
FINELY GRATED ZEST OF 2
   ORANGES
265 G (9¼ OZ/1¾ CUPS) PLAIN
   (ALLPURPOSE) FLOUR
1 TEASPOON BAKING POWDER
1 TEASPOON BICARBONATE OF
   SODA (BAKING SODA)

SYRUP
JUICE OF 2 ORANGES
JUICE OF 1½ LEMONS
175 G (¾ CUP) CASTER (SUPERFINE)
   SUGAR

Preheat the oven to 160°C (315°F). Grease and line a 24 cm (9½ inch) springform cake tin.

In an electric mixer, cream the butter and sugar until pale and creamy. Beat in the egg yolks, sour cream and zest. Sift the flour with the baking powder and bicarbonate of soda, then fold in to the butter mixture.

In a separate bowl, whisk the egg whites until stiff but not dry. Add the whites to the butter and flour mixture and carefully fold together to combine. Pour into the prepared tin and bake for 1 hour, or until a skewer inserted in the cake comes out clean.

About 5 minutes before the cake is ready, make the syrup by combining the juices and sugar in a small saucepan. Bring to the boil, stirring from time to time, until the sugar has dissolved, then simmer until thickened and sticky, about 10–15 minutes.

Remove the cake from the oven, allow to stand for 10 minutes and then pour the boiling syrup over the top. Allow to cool before removing from the tin.

Serves 10

Leah was born in Hong Kong in 1936 to Russian-born parents. They lived in Canton, stateless, travelling to Hong Kong for the birth of each baby, to ensure the child had a passport. The family immigrated to Sydney shortly after the Second World War where Leah finished school, then married young. Quickly starting a family, her skills in the kitchen were self taught and sometimes experimental.

Sunday evening dinners in Chinatown, with up to 30 family members, became a tradition, now continued by her children.

Later moving to South Africa, her partner, Alan, always said there was no point eating in restaurants; Leah cooked better food than could be found anywhere.

Leah loved calling her children anytime and anywhere to discuss a favourite restaurant or dish. Even after her devastating leukaemia diagnosis, she still scoured the paper every week, insisting on eating the final family Chinese dinner at the latest hip Chinese incarnation in Sydney. Leah passed away in 2012.

DINKIE WASSERMAN

In the 1950s, when eating a kranzkuchen for the first time at a friend's house, my husband, Basil, declared, 'This is the sort of cake I like.' From that moment on it became a permanent part of my repertoire. My two remaining sons, their friends, my friends and my grandkids know me for my kranzkuchen. Most have grown up eating it; it is a cake that has been with me through every milestone in my life and my granddaughter Nicole tells me I am 'as sweet as the cherries on top'.

Kranzkuchen

225 G (8 OZ/1½ CUPS) PLAIN (ALL-PURPOSE) FLOUR

75 G (2¾ OZ/½ CUP) SELF-RAISING FLOUR

2 TEASPOONS BAKING POWDER

1½ TABLESPOONS CASTER (SUPERFINE) SUGAR

60 G (2¼ OZ) UNSALTED BUTTER, AT ROOM TEMPERATURE

PINCH OF SALT

1 EGG

250 ML (1 CUP) PURE CREAM (35% FAT)

150–300 G (½–1 CUP) SMOOTH APRICOT JAM (DEPENDING ON HOW SWEET YOU LIKE IT)

1½ TABLESPOONS CINNAMON SUGAR (SEE NOTE)

250 G (1½ CUPS) MIXED CURRANTS, SULTANAS (GOLDEN RAISINS) AND RAISINS

MILK, FOR GLAZING

Preheat the oven to 180°C (350°F/Gas 4). Line a large baking tray.

Using a pastry cutter or your fingers, mix the flours, baking powder, sugar, butter and salt together until the mixture resembles coarse crumbs.

Mix the egg with the cream and pour into the flour mixture. Using a knife, bring the mixture together to form a soft but rollable dough. Add a little more plain flour if it is too sticky.

Tip the dough onto a floured board. Using a rolling pin, roll out the dough to form a rough oval about 35 x 45 cm (14 x 17¾ inches) in size. Spread the entire surface with the jam, sprinkle on the cinnamon sugar and then top with the dried fruit.

Roll up, starting at the top (the wider side), to make a long log and pinch the ends together. Place the log carefully onto the prepared tray. Bring the ends down so that the log is now a horseshoe or half-moon shape. With a knife, make five or so vertical slits on the outside rounded edge. Paint the top with the milk and bake until golden brown and cooked through, about 45 minutes.

ICING

160 g (1 cup) ICING
   (CONFECTIONERS') SUGAR
¼ TEASPOON WATER
JUICE OF ½ LEMON,
   APPROXIMATELY 25 ML
60 g (¼ CUP) GLACÉ CHERRIES
   (OPTIONAL)

When completely cool, make the icing. Mix the sugar, water and lemon juice to a smooth paste.

Pour the icing over the top of the log and allow to drip down the sides. Decorate with the glacé cherries, if desired.

Serves 12–16

NOTE: To make the cinnamon sugar, combine 1 tablespoon ground cinnamon with 1 cup caster (superfine) sugar.

Photos on page 234–5

DINKIE WASSERMAN

Growing up, I never entered the kitchen. It was only after I married in 1953 that I started to cook. My husband, Basil, asked that I please not make the food of my parents' heritage (English, South African) but rather the food of his mother's family who had come from Russia and Lithuania. There began lessons from my mother-in-law, Granny Lily, who was the most wonderful cook. I was 21 at the time and remember watching her in the kitchen, following each step closely and measuring every single ingredient after Granny had put in her 'pinch of this' and 'dash of that'.

Cooking became a part of who I was; preparing food for Basil, our three sons and friends as well as catering for the Johannesburg Waverly Synagogue. Since I immigrated to Sydney in 2002 I have cherished my assigned role in preparing the meal before the Yom Kippur fast for my son and my three grandchildren every year.

Although I don't spend as much time in the kitchen as I used to, when I do bake it is extremely satisfying. I have found solace in the kitchen through all the tough and challenging moments of my life, and through the happier times as well. I proudly baked many cakes for my recent 80th birthday party and what a pleasure it was to watch everyone enjoy them so much.

{Kranzkuchen}

When friends heard that Mom had made her hot milk sponge, they were over in a flash and even after all these years, my school friends all still remember it well. To make a chocolate version, add ¼ cup cocoa powder into the cake mix and then ice with a chocolate ganache (page 59).

Hot milk sponge

4 EGGS, AT ROOM TEMPERATURE
430 G (15¼ OZ/2 SCANT CUPS) CASTER
    (SUPERFINE) SUGAR
1 TEASPOON VANILLA EXTRACT
300 G (10½ OZ/2 CUPS) PLAIN (ALL-
    PURPOSE) FLOUR
1 TABLESPOON BAKING POWDER
250 ML (1 CUP) MILK
125 G (4½ OZ) BUTTER
75 G (¼ CUP) JAM
185 ML (¾ CUP) THICKENED
    (WHIPPING) CREAM, WHIPPED
    UNTIL FIRM
40 G (¼ CUP) ICING SUGAR, FOR
    DUSTING

Preheat the oven to 170°C (325°F/Gas 3). Grease and line two 20 cm (8 inch) round cake tins.

Beat the eggs and sugar until light and fluffy. Add the vanilla.

Sift the flour and baking powder together and fold into the egg mixture.

Put the milk and butter in a small saucepan and as soon as it starts to boil, fold into the cake batter.

Divide the batter between the prepared tins and bake for 25–30 minutes, or until golden brown and spongy to touch when pressed lightly. Be careful not to overcook.

Allow the cakes to cool slightly before turning out onto a wire rack. When completely cool, sandwich them together with the jam and whipped cream, and sift the icing sugar on top.

Serves 8–10

I must have had a natural love for cooking from a young age, as I was preparing food when my friends of the same age were not into it at all. My mom always told me, 'If you can read, you can cook or bake.' So, as a very young girl I could always be found in the kitchen experimenting.

I grew up in a small town on the Western Cape of South Africa called Vredenburg, a transportation and commercial hub of the West Coast. My dad was an accountant for a large fishing company and I lived there until I got married. My husband and I then lived in Saskatchewan, Canada, before immigrating to Australia in 1996. The Gold Coast is now home and we are so happy living here.

I can't imagine a life without cooking. It was so ingrained in me by my mom. Since I could read my very first cookbook, preparing and sharing food is still such a joy.

My mom always made these buttermilk rusks and though I have tried many different recipes, these are by far my favourite and enjoyed by all who taste them. Traditionally South African, they can be enjoyed at any time, even breakfast, and are often dunked into a cup of tea. They are great to take on car trips and can be kept for a long time in an airtight container.

Buttermilk rusks

500 G (1 LB 2 OZ/3⅓ CUPS) **PLAIN (ALL-PURPOSE) FLOUR**
3 TEASPOONS BAKING POWDER
150 G (5½ OZ/⅔ CUP) **CASTER (SUPERFINE) SUGAR**
165 G (5¾ OZ) **UNSALTED BUTTER, CHOPPED, AT ROOM TEMPERATURE**
1 EGG, LIGHTLY BEATEN
170 ML (⅔ CUP) **BUTTERMILK**

Start this recipe the day before.

Preheat the oven to 160°C (315°F/Gas 2–3). Line a baking tin, approximately 27 x 17 cm (10¾ x 6¾ inches).

Sift the flour and baking powder into a bowl, add the sugar and mix. Mix in the butter with your fingertips until the mixture resembles coarse crumbs. Add the egg and the buttermilk and mix with a spoon until it comes together to form a smooth dough.

Divide the dough into 10 pieces (each piece about 1 handful) and roll each piece between your hands to form a small rough log, about 7.5 x 5 cm (3 x 2 inches). Place the logs side by side in two rows in the prepared tin, touching each other. Bake for 45 minutes until golden brown, or until a skewer inserted into a log comes out clean. Remove the logs from the oven and allow to cool.

Reduce the oven temperature to 100°C (200°F). Line a large baking tray. Separate and cut each log lengthways into 2 or 3 pieces. Place on the prepared tray and return to the oven for about 5 hours, or until dry and hard. Turn the oven off, leaving the rusks there to further harden as they cool down, preferably overnight.

Makes about 20–30 rusks
Store in an airtight container for up to 1 month

My mum, Sue Nuyten, got this recipe from her sister when she first married over 50 years ago, and has been making them ever since. She loves giving batches away to friends – who love her for them. My boys and I love dunking them in our tea. – Paula Horwitz

Dutch spice biscuits

225 G (8 oz/1½ cups) PLAIN (ALL-PURPOSE) FLOUR

125 G (4½ oz) BUTTER, AT ROOM TEMPERATURE

230 G (8½ oz/1 cup) SUGAR

1 HEAPED TEASPOON MIXED SPICE

1 TABLESPOON GROUND GINGER

½ TEASPOON GROUND CINNAMON

1 EGG, LIGHTLY BEATEN

1 TEASPOON BICARBONATE OF SODA (BAKING SODA)

1 TABLESPOON GOLDEN SYRUP (LIGHT TREACLE)

2 TEASPOONS MILK

Preheat the oven to 140°C (275°F/Gas 1). Line a baking tray.

Rub the flour and butter together in a bowl. Add the sugar, mixed spice, ginger and cinnamon and mix well. Stir through the egg, bicarbonate of soda, golden syrup and milk. Knead everything together to form a smooth dough. Alternatively, mix all the ingredients together in an electric mixer.

Take teaspoons of the dough and roll into balls. Place on the prepared baking tray 5 cm (2 inches) apart. Press down lightly with a fork. Bake for 40 minutes, or until golden.

Makes 40 biscuits
Store in an airtight container for up to 2 weeks

Read Paula's story on page 16

I enjoy cooking but I'm not a person who likes sweets. I love this birdseed slice because it is not too sweet, quite healthy and very easy to make in large quantities. It lasts for weeks and can be eaten for breakfast, a snack or dessert. This recipe originally came from Shelley Watson and I have changed it over the years to suit my taste. A nice substituion is ½ cup slivered almonds instead of the dates.

Birdseed slice

140 G (5 oz/4 cups) SPECIAL K OR
    CORNFLAKES
65 G (½ CUP) SESAME SEEDS
75 G (½ CUP) PEPITAS (PUMPKIN SEEDS)
70 G (½ CUP) SUNFLOWER SEEDS
90 G (½ CUP) DRIED CRANBERRIES
90 G (½ CUP) CHOPPED PITTED
    DRIED DATES
200 G (7 oz) LIGHT SWEETENED
    CONDENSED MILK

Preheat the oven to 180°C (350°F/Gas 4). Line one large or two small baking trays.

Place all the dry ingredients in a large bowl. Drizzle on the condensed milk, mixing gently until combined.

Pour onto the prepared tray, using a spatula, to spread to approximately 1–2 cm (½–¾ inch) thick, then use a potato masher to press the slice flat. Bake for 7 minutes, reduce the temperature to 140°C (275°F/Gas 1) and bake for another 8–10 minutes, or until light golden brown in the middle and at the edges.

Allow to cool. Break up in large pieces to serve.

Serves 16

I grew up in Melbourne in a traditional Jewish home with my Eastern European parents, for whom cooking was an essential and much-loved part of the daily routine. I have now lived in Sydney for more than 25 years, where I have brought up my family, and cooking has become an integral part of my life as well.

Now that our children have grown up, I don't seem to do the everyday cooking as much, so I enjoy any opportunity to put on extravagant Shabbat dinners. I spend hours in the kitchen preparing feasts for my guests. My late mother-in-law, Agi, taught me some classic Hungarian dishes from her home country, but I could never bring myself to use as much butter and sour cream as the recipes called for.

I have compiled a handwritten scrapbook of my favourite recipes and am constantly adding new finds and amending and updating old recipes. It has become my daughters' and my cooking bible with recipes from family, friends, magazines and books. Each time we spend the day together in the kitchen planning and preparing a yomtov or simcha feast, I know I have passed my love of cooking down the line.

Tradition

Food brings tradition into my home. I draw on much-loved recipes for the never-ending cycle of Jewish festivals, when my extended family gathers around a dining table laden with evocative dishes. Whether feeding them sizzling golden potato latkes on Chanukah or baking my little syrupy honey cakes for gifts on Rosh Hashanah, there's nothing I love more than serving up a generous portion of tradition.

Merelyn x

Recipes

{Simple chicken soup}

This is the soup we sell at the deli. It is made with lots of chicken bones, creating a clear, rich soup which jellies when cold. It is best served piping hot with kreplach or matzo balls.

Simple chicken soup

1 X MEDIUM CHICKEN, CUT INTO
    PIECES
2 KG (4 LB 8 OZ) CHICKEN
    CARCASSES
2 CARROTS, PEELED
1 LARGE ONION, UNPEELED AND
    QUARTERED
2–3 DILL STEMS (OPTIONAL)
SEA SALT AND FRESHLY GROUND
    BLACK PEPPER

Start this recipe the day before serving.

Wash the chicken and the bones under cold running water. Put them in a stockpot or very large saucepan along with the other ingredients. Pour in enough cold water to just cover, around 3–4 litres (12–16 cups). Bring to the boil. Skim off the scum that rises to the surface, partially cover with a lid, reduce heat to medium–low, and continue to cook at a light boil for 1½–2 hours. Allow to cool slightly for 30 minutes before removing the bones and straining the soup, discarding everything except the carrot.

Add salt and pepper to taste to the soup. Allow to cool and refrigerate overnight.

The next day, skim off the fat from the top of the soup.

Reheat the soup to serve, tasting for seasoning and flavour. If the flavour is not strong enough, bring to the boil and reduce to reach the desired taste, and if the flavour is too strong, add some water.

Serve within 3 days or freeze for up to 3 months. Serve with the reserved carrots and matzo balls (facing page).

Makes 3–4 litres (12–16 cups)

Photo on page 246

Matzo balls are matzo meal dumplings eaten in chicken soup, traditionally served at Pesach, although they are also enjoyed all year round. This is my recipe, which took me about four years to perfect. When you have orders for 7000 matzo balls at Pesach, you don't want to make any mistakes.

Balaclava Deli's matzo balls

9 EGGS, SEPARATED

375 G (13 OZ/3 HEAPED CUPS) COARSE
  MATZO MEAL

185 ML (¾ CUP) VEGETABLE OIL

125 ML (½ CUP) WATER

1 TEASPOON SALT, OR TO TASTE

FRESHLY GROUND BLACK PEPPER

In an electric mixer, whisk the egg whites until stiff peaks form.

In a separate bowl, beat the egg yolks lightly and mix with the matzo meal, oil, water, salt and pepper. Add this mixture spoon by spoon to the egg whites, whisking after each addition. Taste and season generously. Set aside for 30 minutes, giving it a light fold through after 15 minutes.

Bring a stockpot or very large saucepan of well-salted water to the boil.

With wet hands, and without pressing too firmly, lightly roll the matzo meal mixture into smooth walnut-sized balls and drop into the boiling water. After the last ball has been dropped in, continue to boil for 20 minutes. Remove the pot from the heat and allow the balls to cool in the water. When ready to serve, remove with a slotted spoon and reheat in chicken soup (facing page).

Makes 50–60 matzo balls

Photo on page 246

My parents were refugees from the Ukraine and Russia, settling in Tashkent, Uzbekistan, in 1941.

I always wanted to help out at home as my parents both worked, so I started cooking when I was about nine years old. From that moment on, it was a joy for me to be in the kitchen. I dreamed one day I would be a chef, but as my parents wished, I finished university with a degree in mathematics and a PhD in economics before I chased any dreams.

I married my schoolmate Pavel and when things declined in Tashkent after the 1990 civil war, we moved to Melbourne with my extended family. It was difficult in the beginning but as soon as I found a job in an Italian restaurant, things started to turn around. This was a perfect chance for a new beginning.

In 1998 we bought The Balaclava Deli in Carlisle Street, in the heart of Jewish Melbourne. It came with the most lovely customers, who over the years grew to trust and love us. I am proud that I have served three generations – grandparents, parents and now their children – who come not just for food, but to share stories, lives and simchas. They are all part of my family. (See also Lena's Russian blintzes on page 202.)

My mum, Sylvie Collins, often makes this standout jam for Pesach as we love it schmeared on matzo. Beetroot is an unusual ingredient for jam but cooks down beautifully to make this dark, sticky and rich jam studded with almonds.
– Jacqui Israel

Beetroot jam

4 LARGE (700 G/1 LB 9 OZ) **BEETROOT**
   (BEETS)
880 G (4 CUPS) **SUGAR**
250 ML (1 CUP) **WATER**
200 ML (¾ CUP PLUS 1 TABLESPOON)
   LEMON JUICE
2 TEASPOONS GROUND GINGER
125 G (1 SCANT CUP) **ALMONDS,**
   CHOPPED

Start this recipe the day before serving.

Peel and grate the beetroot. Combine with the sugar in a bowl, cover with plastic wrap and allow to stand overnight.

The next day, transfer the beetroot and sugar to a saucepan. Add the water and lemon juice and bring to the boil over medium heat, stirring occasionally. Simmer gently over low heat for 2½ hours, stirring from time to time, or until there is no more liquid and the jam has become thick, taking care not to burn it.

Meanwhile, sterilise two 375 ml (1½ cup) jars (see note).

Add the ginger and nuts to the jam and simmer for 5 more minutes. Immediately pour into the hot sterilised jars and seal. Allow to cool before serving.

Makes 2 x 375 ml (13 oz) jars
Store in the fridge for up to 3 months

NOTE: To sterilise jars, preheat the oven to 180°C (350°F/Gas 4). Wash the jars and lids in hot, soapy water. Rinse well. Place the jars upright on a baking tray and put in the oven for 10 minutes. Meanwhile, boil the lids in a saucepan of water for 10 minutes. Use tongs to remove the lids and place them upside down on a clean tea towel (dish towel).

Read Jacqui's story on page 16

{Sephardi charoset (left); beetroot jam (right)}

Charoset *is a dish traditionally eaten at the Pesach table. This recipe was originally my mother-in-law's and was passed down to me. This jam-like* charoset *makes a wonderful gift at Pesach and when placed in sterilised jars can last six months or more in the fridge. It is also delicious spread on matzo or crackers, or simply as an accompaniment to cheese.*

Sephardi charoset

500 G (3 CUPS) PITTED DRIED
  DATES
500 G (3 CUPS) SULTANAS (GOLDEN
  RAISINS)
2 LARGE APPLES
2 LARGE ORANGES
500 G (2¼ CUPS) SUGAR
1 HEAPED CUP WALNUTS OR
  ALMONDS, CHOPPED

Start this recipe the day before.

Sterilise 5 x 100 ml (3½ fl oz) jars (see note on page 250).

Wash the dates and sultanas three times with hot water to remove scum. Cover with hot water and allow them to soak overnight, covered with plastic wrap.

The next day, core the apples, quarter them and then halve the pieces again, so that each apple is cut into 8. Wash the oranges well, leave the skin on and cut into small pieces, removing any pips.

Drain the dates and sultanas. Place all the fruit and sugar into a large saucepan. Bring to the boil, then cook slowly over low heat, stirring from time to time, until the mixture is soft, especially the oranges, about 1½ to 2 hours. You do not need to add any liquid. Purée the fruit using a stick blender or food processor.

Pour the *charoset* into the prepared jars and top with the chopped nuts. Seal the jars.

Makes 5 x 100 ml (3½ oz) jars

Photo on page 251

In January 1951 it took my family three and a half days on various BOAC flights to arrive in Australia from Egypt, each night landing and staying in a different hotel before continuing our journey.

It was providence that my mother became best friends with my future mother-in-law. One woman said, 'I have a daughter', the other, 'I have a son', and they arranged a successful shidduch. *Bert and I have now been married for almost 50 years.*

Both mothers were exceptionally good and clever cooks. Jeannette Danon, being Sephardi, cooked with a Spanish–Italian influence while my mother Sabina Carpenter's Ashkanazi roots gave me a Polish–Austrian influence. Both taught me the secrets that had been handed down from mother to daughter; a tradition I have continued with my own children. I have been demonstrating some easy recipes to our young grandchildren and they do enjoy helping me in the kitchen. I have always enjoyed cooking, particularly the art that is involved with every dish.

During the festival of Chanukah, it is traditional to eat fried food. We celebrate the 'miracle of the oil' from when the first temple in Jerusalem was destroyed over 2000 years ago. There was only enough ritual oil to light the sacred candle for one day, but miraculously it lasted for eight days – until the oil was able to be replenished. The most popular Chanukah dish at our house is potato latkes, similar to roesti, which have many incarnations, the simplest of which is here.

Potato latkes

600 G (1 LB 5 OZ) DESIREE (OR
  FRYING) POTATOES
2 EGGS, LIGHTLY BEATEN
1 HEAPED TABLESPOON PLAIN
  (ALL-PURPOSE) FLOUR (OPTIONAL)
SEA SALT AND FRESHLY GROUND
  BLACK PEPPER
250 ML (1 CUP) VEGETABLE OIL

Peel and grate the potatoes. Place in a colander for 15 minutes to drain. Squeeze the grated potato with your hands to remove any liquid. Wrap and then wring the potato in a tea towel (dish towel) or paper towel to remove any residual liquid.

Tip the potato into a large bowl. Add the eggs and flour, if using, then season generously with salt and pepper. Mix well.

Add enough oil to a large frying pan to reach a depth of about 5 mm–1 cm (¼–½ inch). When the oil is hot, carefully add teaspoons of the potato mixture to make small round potato cakes. Flatten them slightly. Fry the latkes over medium heat for a few minutes on each side until golden brown. Drain on paper towel.

Serve hot, with crème fraîche and salmon pastrami (page 24).

Makes about 40 small latkes

Photo on page 254
Read Lisa's story on page 13

{Potato latkes}

{Gefilte fish}

Gefilte fish

FISH STOCK

1–1.2 KG (2 LB 4 OZ–2 LB 12 OZ/ABOUT
    2–3) SNAPPER HEADS AND BONES

1 LARGE BROWN ONION, SKINNED,
    LEFT WHOLE

3 CELERY STALKS, EACH CUT INTO
    THIRDS

1 SWEDE (RUTABAGA), PEELED AND
    QUARTERED

1 PARSNIP, PEELED AND
    QUARTERED

4 CARROTS, PEELED AND EACH
    CUT INTO THIRDS

3 TABLESPOONS SUGAR

1 TABLESPOON SALT

1 SMALL HANDFUL BLACK
    PEPPERCORNS

½ BUNCH FLAT-LEAF (ITALIAN)
    PARSLEY

3 DRIED BAY LEAVES

Gefilte fish is best started at least 2 days before serving. The fish stock is best made a day or two before cooking, and the raw fish mixture is best refrigerated overnight. The cooked balls are served cold, so they need to be chilled after cooking.

First, make the stock. To clean the fish heads and bones, cut off and discard the sharp fins and eyes. Rinse the heads and bones in cold water and clean thoroughly. Place them in a stockpot or very large saucepan with the onion, celery, swede, parsnip and carrot and cover with cold water. Add the sugar and salt and bring to the boil. Skim off the scum that rises to the top. Add the peppercorns, parsley and bay leaves. Cover the pot and simmer gently for 2 hours. Strain and adjust the seasoning to taste. Cool and refrigerate until needed.

Heat the oil in a large frying pan and gently fry half the onion until soft and light golden, about 10 minutes. Set aside to cool.

Using a mincer, mince the fish with both the raw and fried onion and finish with the challah. Omit the challah during Passover. Add the matzo meal, eggs and seasonings to the mixture and mix well. Pour in as much water as needed (up to 1 cup) to lighten the mixture. Cover with plastic wrap and refrigerate for a minimum of 2 hours but preferably overnight, to allow the liquid to be absorbed and the mixture to firm up.

Before you cook all the gefilte fish, cook one small ball to test for seasoning. Put the stock into the stockpot, add the carrot and bring to

I cannot remember a Passover without homemade gefilte fish, first made by my grandmother and then by my mother. My brothers and I were forever stealing the bright orange rounds of carrot off the top of the balls, something my children now do. It is a quintessential Jewish dish usually served as a first course at the Seder or Rosh Hashanah feast and always served with chrain. This is my mum's recipe, which she adapted from my grandmother's and her old friend Judy Marks's versions.
– Natanya Eskin

FISH BALLS

60 ML (¼ CUP) VEGETABLE OIL

6 LARGE ONIONS, CHOPPED

2 KG (4 LB 8 OZ) MIX OF PERCH,
　BREAM AND MULLOWAY (OR
　OTHER WHITE FISH) FILLETS,
　MINCED (GROUND)

1 SLICE CHALLAH, SOAKED
　IN WATER, THEN LIQUID
　SQUEEZED OUT (OMIT THIS
　DURING PESACH)

85 G (⅔ CUP) FINE MATZO MEAL OR
　FRESH BREADCRUMBS

7 EGGS

2 TABLESPOONS SALT

80 G (⅓ CUP) SUGAR

1½ TEASPOONS FRESHLY GROUND
　WHITE PEPPER

250 ML (1 CUP) WATER

2 CARROTS, PEELED AND CUT
　INTO 3 MM (⅛ INCH) DISCS

PREPARED HORSERADISH
　CONDIMENT, FOR SERVING

the boil. With wet hands, make a walnut-sized ball from the mixture and poach it in the stock for a few minutes. Cool, taste and adjust the seasoning in the mixture if necessary.

Using wet hands and a wet spoon, take roughly 2 dessertspoons of mixture, form into balls and drop into the stock. Continue until all the mixture is used. Cook, covered, on a gentle simmer for 45 minutes. Shake the pot gently from time to time to ensure the balls do not stick. Remove the fish balls and carrots with a slotted spoon. Place the fish balls in a dish in one layer and top each one with a slice of carrot. Cool and then cover with plastic wrap. Refrigerate until serving.

Strain the remaining stock and refrigerate. It will cool to form a jelly that can be served with the fish.

Serve with the horseradish on the side.

Makes approximately 45 medium-sized balls

Photo on page 255
Read Natanya's story on page 14

{Chicken tebeet}

LILY WAITSMAN

Childhood memories of my family sharing platters of food in Tel Aviv planted the seed for my deep love of food and family. My parents originally came from Baghdad, and settled in Israel in 1934 when the situation for Iraqi Jews became very difficult.

In those days, knowledge of cooking was simply passed down through generations; there was rarely a recipe to follow. It was really about watching, learning and teaching. I learned from watching my mother, Daisy, and Aunty Violet cook wonderful dishes like kooba bamia *(okra stew with meat dumplings),* sambusa *(triangular filled pastries) and* salona *(sweet and sour fish). Staple foods were important – when I was growing up there wasn't much more than those around. But the joy of having your family in one place, sharing a meal, was paramount.*

I moved to Sydney in 1964 with my husband and eldest son, Alain, and our other children, Andre and Nicole, were born here a few years later. Once I had my own family and saw how much home cooking is truly appreciated, I was inspired to make beautiful meals for my children and hope I have inspired them to do the same for theirs.

This recipe comes from my mother, Daisy. In those days they didn't have an oven, so the slow-cooked dishes were put in the public ovens in the apartment buildings. After synagogue on Saturday, the pot was collected and we would come home to a fragrant hot lunch. I still make it for Friday night dinner and any leftovers make an easy and delicious Saturday lunch. It's one of my daughter Nicole's favourites.

Chicken tebeet

60 ML (¼ CUP) VEGETABLE OIL

1 X 2 KG (4 LB 8 OZ) CHICKEN

2 LARGE ONIONS, CHOPPED

3 TOMATOES, PEELED AND
CHOPPED

2 TEASPOONS TOMATO PASTE
(CONCENTRATED PURÉE)

875 ML (3½ CUPS) WATER

2 TEASPOONS SEA SALT

FRESHLY GROUND BLACK PEPPER

660 G (3 CUPS) BASMATI RICE

1½ TABLESPOONS BAHARAT SPICE
MIX (SEE NOTE), PLUS EXTRA,
FOR SPRINKLING

Choose a flameproof casserole dish that is deep enough to hold the whole chicken surrounded by rice.

Heat the oil in the casserole dish and brown the chicken all over, turning regularly. Set aside. Add the onion and fry over medium heat until pale golden. Add the tomato and tomato paste and stir through. Return the chicken to the dish. Add 500 ml (2 cups) of the water, the salt and pepper and bring to the boil. Simmer, covered, for 30 minutes.

Meanwhile, wash the rice until the water runs clear. Place the rice in a bowl, cover with water and soak until required. The colour of the rice will change to a chalky white.

Remove the chicken from the dish and set aside. Taste the onion and tomato mix and add more salt if necessary.

Preheat the oven to 110°C (225°F/Gas ¼).

Drain the rice and add to the onion and tomato mix with the remaining water. Add the baharat and bring to the boil. Return the chicken to the dish, burying it in the rice. Sprinkle a little extra baharat on top, without stirring. Cover the dish, place in the oven and cook, checking from time to time to ensure it is not burning, for 4 hours. A deep golden crust of rice should form on the bottom and sides of the pan.

To serve, place the chicken in the centre of a large platter. The chicken will fall apart, so you may want to remove some of the smaller bones. Heap the rice around the chicken, carefully arranging any crust on top, if possible.

Serves 6–8

NOTE: Baharat is a Middle Eastern spice blend typically containing salt, pepper, cassia, cloves, coriander seeds and cardamom. It can be found in spice shops and gourmet delicatessens.

Photo on page 259

We always ate this sweet brisket at Pesach and Rosh Hashanah. Originally from my grandmother, who was quite secretive with her recipes, my mother learned it by simply watching and copying. Due to ill health, my mother can no longer cook, but we all think and talk about her when I make this dish. It has a particular sweetness for me that goes far beyond its taste.

Flammen tsimmes brisket

1 TABLESPOON VEGETABLE OIL

2 KG (4 LB 8 OZ) PIECE FRESH BEEF
   BRISKET

2 ONIONS, HALVED AND SLICED
   INTO WEDGES

1 KG (2 LB 4 OZ) WAXY POTATOES
   (SUCH AS KIPFLER), PEELED AND
   THICKLY SLICED

400 G (1¾ CUPS) PITTED PRUNES

SEA SALT AND FRESHLY GROUND
   BLACK PEPPER

175 G (½ CUP) GOLDEN SYRUP (LIGHT
   TREACLE)

2 TABLESPOONS LEMON JUICE

You will need a saucepan large enough to hold the brisket.

Heat the oil in the pan and brown the brisket on both sides. Add the onion, potato, three-quarters of the prunes and 2 teaspoons of salt. Cover with boiling water and half the golden syrup. Bring to the boil, partially cover, then simmer until quite tender, at least 1¼ hours.

Preheat the oven to 180°C (350°F/Gas 4).

Take the meat out of the liquid and place in an ovenproof dish. Strain and reserve the liquid, and spoon the onion, potato and prunes on top of the brisket. Pour enough liquid into the dish so that it comes halfway up the meat. Top with the remaining prunes and golden syrup. Sprinkle over ½ teaspoon of salt and plenty of pepper. Roast, uncovered, basting every 15 minutes or so, for 1–1½ hours, or until the meat is fork tender.

To serve, sprinkle with the lemon juice.

Serves 8

Opposed to the apartheid regime in South Africa in the 1970s, my parents immigrated to Australia. I was only eleven when we arrived, and Sydney has been my home ever since. My parents both enjoy good food and wine but being doctors, they decided it was better for their health to follow a low-fat diet. Notwithstanding, all the women in my family became good cooks, always exchanging recipes and experimenting.

My interest in cooking, though, came from my dad. In the early years Mum, while studying to be a pathologist, was always working weekends so Dad took up cooking as a hobby, making amazing curries and Creole and Cajun dishes – all from scratch. I would spend days with him seeking out hard-to-find herbs and spices. We started cooking together each Sunday and still do so, decades later.

My husband, Hilton, and I have three children. My father's and my passion for cooking now spans three generations, creating a special bond in the kitchen.

Cholent is a traditional dish often made on Fridays and slow cooked all night ready for the next day, for Shabbat lunch. It is an inexpensive hearty stew – full of beans, barley, potato and a little meat – and it feeds a lot of people. Yvonne always makes it with lots of love and patience, going so far as to wake in the night just to check on it. Over the years I have enjoyed many different cholents and this, an old-style Melbourne version, is my favourite. You can add a couple of spoons of paprika for more spice, some chopped carrots for colour or some smoked bones for a rich flavour. – Lauren Fink

Yvonne's cholent

280 G (1 HEAPED CUP) DRIED LIMA BEANS
120 G (½ HEAPED CUP) DRIED RED KIDNEY BEANS
130 G (½ HEAPED CUP) PEARL BARLEY
5 LARGE ONIONS, CHOPPED
60 ML (¼ CUP) VEGETABLE OIL
1 PIECE FRESH BEEF BRISKET, ABOUT 750 G (1 LB 10 OZ)
5 SMALL WAXY POTATOES, PEELED AND QUARTERED
2 PIECES BEEF TOP RIB OR ASADO (CUT ACROSS THE BONE) BEEF RIBS
1½ TABLESPOONS SALT
1 LITRE (4 CUPS) BOILING WATER

Start this recipe 2 days before serving.

You will need at least a 6 litre (24 cup) flameproof casserole dish.

Soak the beans and barley together in a large bowl in plenty of water overnight. The next day, drain and rinse.

Preheat the oven to 130°C (250°F/Gas ½).

Saute the onion in the oil in a frying pan over medium–high heat until golden brown, about 15 minutes. Remove the onion and set aside.

Put the brisket in the bottom of the casserole dish. Divide each of the onion, beans/barley and potato into three. In that order, put one layer of each, then half the top rib, another layer of each, the remaining top rib, the remaining layer of each, finishing with a layer of potato.

Dissolve the salt in the boiling water and pour in the dish. It should come to just under the top layer of potatoes (add more water if necessary). Bring to the boil on the stovetop and then place an open brown paper bag or some baking paper on top of the potato layer and cover with a lid. Bake for 2 hours. Turn the oven down to 100°C (200°F) and cook for a further 20–22 hours, checking from time to time. Alternatively, cook at 150°C (300°F/Gas 2) for 4½ hours. Add more water if it looks like it is drying out too much.

Serves 8–12

Read Lauren's story on page 15

Aunty Myrna made these traditional Rosh Hashanah honeyed carrots each year. I can picture her telling me how it represents the wish for a sweet (thanks to the honey) and prosperous (the carrot 'coins') new year. The recipe calls for butter, but you can use margarine to make it pareve. Our Rosh Hashanah table always has a space for her sweet carrot tzimmes, a dish that I know will be passed down for many generations to come. – Lisa Goldberg

Aunty Myrna's carrot tzimmes

20 CARROTS, PEELED
170 G (¾ CUP) SUGAR
440 G (1¼ CUPS) HONEY
JUICE OF 3 LEMONS
½ TEASPOON GROUND CINNAMON
**SEA SALT AND FRESHLY GROUND
    BLACK PEPPER**
100 G (3½ OZ) BUTTER

Start this recipe 1–2 days before serving.

Cut the carrots into 5 mm (¼ inch) rounds and soak in water for a few hours or overnight.

Drain the carrot, place in a large saucepan and barely cover with water. Bring to the boil and cook for 5 minutes, then add the sugar, honey, lemon juice, cinnamon, salt and pepper and the butter. Cook, uncovered, stirring regularly, over medium–high heat for 1 hour, or until the carrot is glazed and soft, and the water is almost all gone. Season to taste with extra salt, pepper and lemon juice. Refrigerate the carrot until cold or overnight.

When ready to serve, preheat the oven to 200°C (400°F/Gas 6). Put the carrot in an ovenproof dish, cover with foil and bake for 1 hour. Remove the foil for the last 15 minutes so the carrots become glazed and golden.

Serves 20 as a side dish

Read Lisa's story on page 13

MAXINE RICH AND ALI LINZ

SISTERS

Maxine

A mother, two grandmothers, a heritage of women – all talking food. My childhood is infused with the rich memories of smell; the bready scents of kugelhopf welcoming our return from school, the crackle of sizzling oil announcing latkes and schnitzel at the end of the week, and the exciting smells of chilli and garlic heralding family and friends.

From the earliest age, Mum encouraged us to cook too – grating cucumbers and carrots, swooshing hands in sticky fish batter and frying French toast with extra icing sugar. Cake-making was the preserve of Saturday afternoons, when Mum sacrificed her clean kitchen in exchange for the privilege of a rare afternoon nap.

Thanks to my heritage, the ingredients of German, Hungarian and English life peppered many of our meals, while our Polish heritage scored a fleeting look in now and then. For us, food was like our lives – full of diversity, sprinkled with the old and dashed with the new.

Ali

For me, good food is all about feeling loved. My grandmother, Ruth, treasures the cookbook which her mother – my great-grandmother – wrote for her trousseau. Every page is written in old-fashioned German in perfectly manicured handwriting. My mother, by contrast, is a free spirit. She studied at the Cordon Bleu, but when I was a small child she would put a chopping board and knife on the floor so I could happily imitate her chopping garlic, just like she did at the benchtop. Later, I sat on the benchtop, making kugelhopf cakes and soufflés, while she patiently cleaned up my mess. My children now do the same. When I see them coated in meringue mixture, I feel the joy of my childhood again.

Our whole family is food obsessed. Not with fancy haute cuisine, but with food that feeds our souls. The only question anyone in my family will ever ask about where you've been is: 'What did you eat?'

This matzo granola was created years ago in desperation when we had a birthday breakfast celebration for our daughter during Passover. There is only so far yoghurt and fruit can take you when there are no croissants, no cheese pockets and no rich buttered toast! What started off as a birthday treat soon became a Passover family fixture. It also provides a welcome change from tasty but weighty matzo brei!

Matzo granola

6 SHEETS MATZO, BROKEN INTO ROUGH 2 CM (¾ INCH) SQUARES
70 G (¾ CUP) DESICCATED COCONUT
115 G (¾ CUP) WHOLE ALMONDS
80 ML (⅓ CUP) VEGETABLE OIL
175 G (½ CUP) HONEY
¼ TEASPOON SEA SALT
1½ TEASPOONS GROUND CINNAMON
80 G (½ CUP) RAISINS
80 G (½ CUP) DRIED APRICOTS, CHOPPED

Preheat the oven to 180°C (350°F/Gas 4). Line a large baking tray.

Combine the matzo, coconut and almonds in a large bowl, then spread on the prepared tray and bake for 20 minutes, tossing several times.

Meanwhile, stir the oil, honey and salt in a saucepan over medium heat until melted and combined.

In a large bowl, combine the roasted matzo mix with the honey mixture. Toss through the cinnamon. Return to the baking tray and bake for a further 15 minutes, tossing from time to time. Add the raisins and apricots and toss well. Bake for another 5 minutes. Remove from the oven and cool on the tray.

Break up any chunks that are too large. Store in an airtight container for up to two weeks.

Serve with plain yoghurt and stewed fruit or on its own as a crunchy snack.

Makes 5 cups

I'll never forget when my grandmother first tasted my lamb shanks. She professed, 'You could go anywhere with this!', which roughly translates as 'this is the food equivalent of a Harvard MBA!' It's perfect to drop off to someone who needs a bit of cheer or to serve at Friday night dinner. It freezes and reheats well and the leftovers are yum shredded and added to pasta.

Balsamic lamb shanks

40 G (¼ CUP) PLAIN (ALL-PURPOSE) FLOUR, FOR DUSTING

1 TEASPOON SEA SALT

8 SMALL LAMB SHANKS, FRENCH TRIMMED

60 ML (¼ CUP) OLIVE OIL

4 CLOVES GARLIC, CRUSHED

1 TABLESPOON ROSEMARY LEAVES, FINELY CHOPPED

185 ML (¾ CUP) BALSAMIC VINEGAR

250 ML (1 CUP) DRY RED WINE

SEA SALT AND FRESHLY GROUND BLACK PEPPER

6 SMALL RED ONIONS, ABOUT 650 G (1 LB 7 OZ) IN TOTAL

Preheat the oven to 180°C (350°F/Gas 4).

Mix the flour and salt together and lightly coat the lamb shanks.

In a flameproof casserole dish, heat a little olive oil (reserving 1 tablespoon for the next step) and brown the shanks, in batches, over medium heat for about 10 minutes until well coloured, then set aside.

Add the reserved oil, garlic and rosemary to the dish and toss around, scraping the bottom of the dish to get all the nice sticky bits. Stir in the vinegar and wine, bring to the boil, then simmer for 5 minutes.

Return the shanks to the dish, season with salt and pepper, and cover with baking paper and a lid. Put into the oven and cook for 1 hour. Slice each onion into six wedges. Remove the dish from the oven and add the onion. Cook for a further 2 hours, or until fork tender and the meat is falling off the bone. Remove the shanks from the dish and keep warm. Skim the fat off the sauce, then simmer on the stovetop for about 10–15 minutes until the sauce is reduced to a glaze.

Pour the sauce over the shanks to serve.

Delicious served with soft polenta, potato purée or potato and onion gratin (page 175).

Serves 6–8

RUTH BRECKLER

*My family moved from Melbourne to Perth in
1976 when I was fourteen. In our household music
brought the family together. My father played and
taught saxophone and clarinet and my mother was
an accomplished pianist. We often had sing-alongs
around the piano before indulging in Mum's delicious
homemade treats. I learned a lot of recipes from Mum;
she was a simple but good cook.*

*My bobba (paternal grandma), Chaya Kooperman,
rarely wrote down a recipe. Originally from Palestine,
she was known in the Perth community for welcoming
guests with a kosher, traditional Jewish meal. My nana
Doris Crawcour's cooking, on the other hand, was more
English, simple and nutritious, with a lot of the produce
coming from her own garden. Whenever we visited her
in Launceston, we ran out to the veggie patch to pick
what we wanted to eat – home-grown strawberries for
dessert were particularly delicious.*

*Through watching and helping over the years, I
enjoyed learning many of my grandmothers' recipes, and
with my own family, nothing is more satisfying than my
husband and children's smiles when they come home to
the familiar smells permeating the house.*

*I truly believe that cooking enables the generations
before us to live on. I cook with the photos of my late
parents beside me, watching and guiding me as I make
those special dishes. And I hope my children will want to
continue in this family tradition.*

These honey biscuits are very special to me as they originate from my mother, Lynette, and her mother, Doris. This recipe has and always will be a family favourite, and one I never thought I would share. After years of pleasure giving the biscuits as gifts on Rosh Hashanah, my sister Julie and I have decided to pass the recipe on in Mum's memory. They are very sweet, and unique in texture. They store well and can be frozen.

Honey biscuits

60 G (2¼ OZ) UNSALTED BUTTER, AT
ROOM TEMPERATURE
170 G (6 OZ/¾ CUP) CASTER
(SUPERFINE) SUGAR
170 G (6 OZ/½ CUP) HONEY
1 EGG
420 G (15 OZ/3 SCANT CUPS) PLAIN
(ALL-PURPOSE) FLOUR
1 TEASPOON BICARBONATE OF
SODA (BAKING SODA)
½ TEASPOON GROUND CINNAMON
PINCH OF GROUND CLOVES
1 EGG WHITE, LIGHTLY WHISKED,
FOR GLAZING

In an electric mixer, cream the butter and sugar until pale and creamy.

Warm the honey gently in a saucepan or in the microwave until lukewarm, then add to the butter mixture. Add the egg and mix well.

Sift together the flour, bicarbonate of soda, cinnamon and cloves. Beat into the butter mixture on low speed until a soft dough forms. Shape the dough into a ball and cover with plastic wrap. Rest it in the freezer for 1 hour or the fridge for 2–3 hours.

Preheat the oven to 180°C (350°F/Gas 4). Line two baking trays.

Roll out the dough on a lightly floured benchtop to about 5 mm (¼ inch) thick, then cut out shapes with a biscuit cutter and place on the prepared trays, well spaced to allow for spreading. Brush with the egg white and bake for 10–12 minutes, or until golden brown.

Cool on the baking trays. Store in an airtight container for up to 1 month.

Makes about 30 biscuits

Growing up, this dessert was a regular in our house. It is easy to make the day before and is pareve, *so it can be served after any main course. It is delightfully light and fluffy and refreshing on the palate; the perfect finish to a meal.*

Lemon bavarois

6 FRESH LARGE EGGS, SEPARATED

230 G (8½ OZ/1 CUP) CASTER
(SUPERFINE) SUGAR

1 SACHET (3 TEASPOONS) POWDERED
GELATINE

125 ML (½ CUP) BOILING WATER

FINELY GRATED ZEST OF 2
LEMONS

80 ML (⅓ CUP) LEMON JUICE

½ CUP RASPBERRIES, FOR
SERVING

Whisk the egg yolks with half of the sugar until thick and creamy.

Stir the gelatine into the boiling water until dissolved. Stir in the lemon zest and juice, then whisk into the egg yolk mixture. Place in the fridge to thicken, checking and stirring every 10 minutes or so, until the consistency of pouring cream. If it sets too much it will be difficult to fold into the egg whites.

Whisk the egg whites in a large bowl until stiff, not dry, and then whisk in the remaining sugar. Gently fold in the egg yolk mixture with a large metal spoon.

Spoon the bavarois into a large glass serving bowl or divide between six single-serve glasses, cover with plastic wrap and refrigerate for at least 1 hour. To serve, decorate with berries on top.

Serves 6

No matter which city I was in, or who I was having Seder with, I always followed the traditions of making the same dishes that I had grown up with. Without exception, everyone always fell in love with the matzo kugel – and still do. People always come back for seconds – and then ask for the recipe. I imagine that our matzo kugel is now made in many different countries, by friends scattered all over the world. My mother taught me this recipe, given to her by a cousin in the USA.

Matzo kugel

3 SHEETS MATZO

6 EGGS

**115 G (½ CUP) CASTER (SUPERFINE)
SUGAR**

½ TEASPOON GROUND CINNAMON

½ TEASPOON SEA SALT

**80 G (½ CUP) SULTANAS (GOLDEN
RAISINS)**

4 APPLES, GRATED

**115 G (4 OZ) BUTTER OR
MARGARINE, MELTED**

**EXTRA ¼ CUP CASTER (SUPERFINE)
SUGAR, FOR SPRINKLING**

**EXTRA 2 TEASPOONS GROUND
CINNAMON, FOR SPRINKLING**

Preheat the oven to 180°C (350°F/Gas 4). Grease a 20 cm (8 inch) square ovenproof dish.

Break the matzo into rough 3 cm (1¼ inch) square pieces, place in a bowl, cover with water for a minute, then drain and squeeze out any excess water.

In a separate bowl, whisk together the eggs, sugar, cinnamon and salt until well combined. Fold in the sultanas, apple and matzo. Pour into the prepared dish and pour the melted butter or margarine on top, then sprinkle with the extra sugar and cinnamon. Bake for 45 minutes, or until golden brown.

Serves 8

Growing up in Melbourne in a traditional Jewish household and being educated at a Jewish school meant that the yomtovim were very much a part of our routine of family life. For as long as I can remember, Pesach was marked by the arrival after main course of matzo kugel, brandied oranges, chocolate mousse and pavlova. I can go so far as to say that the dessert selection actually told us what festival we were celebrating.

After finishing university I worked as a journalist in London, had my three children in Sydney and then lived the expat life with my family in Asia.

My cooking reflects my life so far. I enjoy to cook the traditional Jewish food to mark the Jewish holidays with my family, but I also love to cook Chinese, Thai and Malaysian dishes. My children also like to mix a traditional Jewish life with the adventures of tasting, travelling and learning about the world. I hope that my experiences have instilled in them the desire to make the most of everything life brings and not waste a single precious minute.

This cheesecake recipe has been a family favourite for over 30 years, having come from a relative in Israel. It's a large cake and is great for feeding a crowd. We normally eat it on the day it's baked, but it sets beautifully overnight in the fridge and becomes easier to slice. Sometimes I fold through a well-drained jar of pitted cherries.

Ricotta cheesecake

7 EGGS

290 G (10¼ OZ/1¼ CUPS) CUP CASTER
   (SUPERFINE) SUGAR

1 KG (2 LB 4 OZ) FRESH RICOTTA
   CHEESE, DRAINED IF WET

250 G (9 OZ) SOUR CREAM

3 TABLESPOONS CUSTARD
   POWDER

1½ TABLESPOONS CORNFLOUR
   (CORNSTARCH)

¾ TEASPOON BAKING POWDER

2 TABLESPOONS VEGETABLE OIL

FINELY GRATED ZEST OF 1 LEMON

Preheat the oven to 180°C (350°F/Gas 4). Grease and line a 28 cm (11 inch) springform cake tin or a 24 cm (9½ inch) square cake tin.

Using an electric mixer, whisk the eggs and sugar until light and fluffy. Add the cheese and beat until smooth, then add the remaining ingredients and beat until well combined. Pour into the prepared tin and bake for 1 hour, or until golden and puffy. The cake will rise during baking, then fall once cooled.

Serves 12–16

I was born in Sydney to an English mother and Hungarian father, and each of their mothers gave me my earliest memories of food. I remember when my English grandmother would play different, made-up games to try and get me to eat. She would put a slice of apple in front of me and then would turn around and start singing. When she looked back to see the apple was gone, she was always so happy. As a young girl, I was inspired watching my grandmother make her special nockedle *(dumplings) and other Hungarian specialties.*

As soon as I was old enough, I entered the kitchen to test out my skills. My sister and I spent our teenage Saturday nights experimenting with all types of food while our parents were out. We had such fun planning and cooking together and watching movies while we ate all our spoils. Of course our parents came home to a spotless kitchen, completely unaware of the mess we had made just hours before!

While the foods we eat keep changing over the years, I still love experimenting and trying new recipes, and it is such a thrill to have everyone in the extended family enjoy what has been prepared. In my experience, good food leads to good conversations and good times.

I learned this recipe from Aunty Helen, who was like a mother to me. I watched her cook and she simply told me what to do. This cake is always a success, and still, to this day, reminds me of her. I bake many of these cakes to give to my children and grandchildren each year for Pesach.

Flourless nutcake

8 EGGS, SEPARATED

200 G (7 OZ/HEAPED ¾ CUP) CASTER (SUPERFINE) SUGAR

230 G (8½ OZ) BEST-QUALITY DARK CHOCOLATE, GRATED

230 G (8½ OZ/2⅓ CUPS) GROUND WALNUTS OR HAZELNUTS

¼ CUP ICING SUGAR, FOR DUSTING

Preheat the oven to 180°C (350°F/Gas 4). Grease and line a 26 cm (10¼ inch) springform cake tin.

Using an electric mixer, whisk the egg whites until soft peaks form, then slowly add the sugar and continue to whisk until thick and glossy. Add the egg yolks, one by one, beating well after each addition. Gently fold in the chocolate and nuts.

Pour the mixture into the prepared tin and bake for 45 minutes, or until a skewer inserted into the middle comes out clean. The cake will dip a little in the middle when it comes out of the oven.

Cool in the tin. Dust with icing sugar to serve.

Serves 10

Born in 1927 in Czechoslovakia, I was an only child in a family who had lived there for generations. During my protected early childhood, I didn't know anything about food and I never went in the kitchen, but I do have a delightful memory of my grandmother making delicious mushrooms with cream, freshly picked from the forest.

The war changed everything – I was the only one in my family to survive. One of 61 orphans on the SS Derna who came to Australia in 1948 to start a new life, I soon married in 1949. Family meant everything to my husband and me, and it was his two aunts in Sydney who taught me so much in the kitchen. Aunty Helen was a very 'rich' cook, always making mouth-watering meats, fresh cucumber salads and beautiful cakes. Not one to ever follow a recipe, my passion for food grew from necessity; I had three children and a husband, and I had to learn.

My best friend, Esther Fiszman, and I also experimented in the kitchen together. She knew more than I did, even teaching me how to make more difficult things like gefilte fish. Today I am the very proud matriarch of four generations and it gives me such great pleasure to prepare the food for my family that they love to eat.

These bite-sized cakes are actually biscuits dipped in honey syrup. They take a bit of patience to make but keep for ages, so you can make them the week before Rosh Hashanah. They are perfect as a gift or to serve for afternoon tea.

Little honey cakes

450 G (1 LB/3 CUPS) PLAIN (ALL-PURPOSE) FLOUR

1 TEASPOON BICARBONATE OF SODA (BAKING SODA)

2 TEASPOONS GROUND CINNAMON

½ TEASPOON GROUND CLOVES

½ TEASPOON FRESHLY GRATED NUTMEG

PINCH OF SEA SALT

250 ML (1 CUP) LIGHT OLIVE OIL

165 G (5¾ OZ/¾ CUP) CASTER (SUPERFINE) SUGAR

60 ML (¼ CUP) SWEET SACRAMENTAL WINE OR PORT

FINELY GRATED ZEST OF 1 ORANGE

STRAINED JUICE OF 1 ORANGE, ABOUT 80 ML (⅓ CUP)

50 G (⅓ CUP) PISTACHIO NUTS, TOASTED AND FINELY CHOPPED

HONEY SYRUP

½ VANILLA BEAN, SPLIT LENGTHWAYS

350 G (1 CUP) HONEY

100 G (½ CUP, FIRMLY PACKED) LIGHT BROWN SUGAR

FINELY GRATED ZEST AND JUICE OF 1 SMALL LEMON

1 CINNAMON STICK

Preheat the oven to 200°C (400°F/Gas 6). Line two baking trays.

For the honey syrup, scrape the seeds from the vanilla bean into a saucepan, add the bean and the remaining ingredients. Slowly bring to the boil, reduce the heat and simmer for 5 minutes.

Sift the flour, bicarbonate of soda, spices and salt into a large bowl.

In a separate bowl, whisk the oil and sugar until well combined, then stir in the wine or port and orange zest and juice.

Gradually pour the oil mixture into the dry ingredients and mix to form a rough dough. Place in the bowl of an electric mixer and, using the dough hook, beat for 5 minutes until smooth, shiny and glutinous, adding extra flour if the dough is too sticky.

Roll the mixture into small walnut-sized balls and place 3 cm (1¼ inches) apart on the prepared baking trays. Lightly flatten each ball with the back of a spoon to make a slight indent and bake for 12 minutes, or until firm.

Remove the vanilla bean and cinnamon stick from the warm syrup, pour into a shallow dish and soak the cakes in the syrup for 30 seconds on each side. Using two forks, lift the cakes from the syrup and place on a wire rack positioned over a tray. Sprinkle with the pistachios and allow to stand for 1 hour.

The cakes will keep in an airtight container for 2–3 weeks.

Makes 50–55 mini cakes

Read Merelyn's story on page 14

These delicious pop-in-your-mouth morsels were always on our Pesach table. A family favourite, traditionally formed as little pyramids, they were quickly eaten and requested regularly. Nana Rene made them, then my mum Sylvie, and now my daughter Lexi and I make them. They are perfect at any time of year.

Coconut macaroons

3¼ CUPS DESICCATED (290 G) OR
  SHREDDED (245 G) COCONUT
155 G (⅔ CUP) CASTER (SUPERFINE)
  SUGAR
2 EGGS, LIGHTLY WHISKED

Preheat the oven to 180°C (350°F/Gas 4). Line a large baking tray.

Prepare a bowl of cold water for wetting your hands.

Mix the ingredients thoroughly until the mixture holds together. With wet hands, press lightly and shape into walnut-sized balls. Place on the prepared tray and bake for 20–25 minutes, or until brown on the outside edges.

Makes 30 macaroons
Store in an airtight container for up to 2 weeks

Read Jacqui's story on page 16

JUSTINE COHEN

This doughnut recipe evolved from a holiday years ago with our cousins. That year, Chanukah and New Year's Eve coincided. Planning our New Year's party, we decided we needed a very large number of sufganiot to help celebrate. Not having any recipes on me, I said I'd have a go at making one up that could produce more than 100 hot and crispy doughnuts for the party. This is the result.

Sufganiot

125 ML (½ CUP) MILK

250 ML (1 CUP) WATER

70 ML (3 ½ TABLESPOONS) VEGETABLE
   OIL

1 EGG

½ TEASPOON SEA SALT

1 TABLESPOON CASTER (SUPERFINE)
   SUGAR

300 G (10½ OZ/2 CUPS) PLAIN (ALL-
   PURPOSE) FLOUR

1½ SACHETS (10 G/3 TEASPOONS)
   ACTIVE DRIED YEAST

VEGETABLE OIL, FOR FRYING

1 CUP CINNAMON SUGAR
   (SEE NOTE)

Place the milk, water, oil, egg, salt, sugar, flour and yeast in the bowl of an electric mixer. Whisk on low until combined, then turn up to medium–high and beat for several minutes until the mixture is glutinous and shiny.

Leave to stand for 1 hour, or up to several hours in the fridge.

To cook the doughnuts, pour the oil to a depth of 10 cm (4 inches) in a large saucepan and heat over medium heat to 180°C (350°F), or until a cube of bread turns golden brown in 15 seconds. Use two soup spoons to shape a doughnut; one to scoop the mixture out of the bowl, one to scrape it into the hot oil. Test one doughnut to check the oil temperature is correct; it should be golden brown after about 2–3 minutes on each side. Fry in batches of 3–4 doughnuts to not crowd the pan. Gently flip using a fork and when cooked, remove with a slotted spoon. Drain on paper towel.

Toss the doughnuts in the cinnamon sugar and serve immediately.

Makes 18–20 doughnuts

NOTE: To make the cinnamon sugar, combine 2 teaspoons ground cinnamon with 1 cup caster (superfine) sugar.

Read Justine's story on page 105

BARBARA KRELL

My husband and I had each travelled the globe before we met, married and then immigrated from South Africa to the beautiful city of Adelaide, over 30 years ago. I was born in Benoni to parents whose families had long before migrated to South Africa from Lithuania and England. My nomadic nature is hereditary; my family moved from place to place, always in search of better opportunities. Having caught the roving bug, I set out as soon as I could to explore the world. Wherever I went, I took with me fond memories of the enchantment of cooking.

I still remember Saturday afternoons in Port Elizabeth when my mother would head into the kitchen, take down her recipe books and browse for something exciting to make for tea. From those magic pages she would conjure up scones, cakes and other goodies; bright pink coconut ice, condensed milk fudge, and peppermint fondant. I can never smell peppermint without thinking of those Saturdays.

Living in Zimbabwe, our Pesach supplies had to come from South Africa, so we would put in our special Pesach order every year at our local Jewish supermarket. The item that we waited for with the greatest excitement was the pletzlach, a sticky, tart, dried-apricot sweet. Over the years their recipe changed and my mother decided it was time to make her own. I remember standing beside her, watching as she stirred and stirred the apricots and then I would shift my gaze to the kitchen window at the pawpaw tree that never gave pawpaws, but that we kept just in case one day it would.

Once Mum started making her own pletzlach, *Pesach was never Pesach without it. For my own two children, Pesach is never Pesach without it either, and each time I make it, it brings my darling departed mother back into my life and back into my kitchen. I relive the memory of standing next to her at the stove and watching her transform a gooey sticky mixture into apricot heaven. Choose tart dried apricots for this recipe, not the sweet Turkish variety.*

1 KG (2 LB 4 OZ) DRIED APRICOTS

1.32 KG (6 CUPS) SUGAR

150 G (1 CUP) BLANCHED ALMONDS, CHOPPED (OPTIONAL)

1–2 CUPS CASTER (SUPERFINE) SUGAR, FOR COATING

Start this recipe the day before serving.

Put the dried apricots in a heavy-based saucepan with enough water to just cover (approximately 3 cups). Bring to the boil, then simmer until the fruit is really soft and the water has boiled away, about 30 minutes. Remove from the heat and purée with a stick blender or mash with a wooden spoon until smooth (small bits of apricot in the mixture are fine).

Prepare a large wooden board by dampening with water.

Add the sugar to the apricot purée. Bring to the boil and simmer over medium heat, stirring constantly with a wooden spoon to avoid burning or catching. Continue to do so for about 30–40 minutes until the colour darkens and the purée thickens and starts to leave the side of the pan when stirred. Reduce the heat to low if it is catching on the bottom. To test if it is ready, a teaspoonful dropped into a glass of cold water will form a small ball. Remove the pan from the heat and stir in the chopped nuts if you are using them. Check the board is still wet, then, working quickly, tip the fruit onto the board and spread out with a palette knife.

Leave to dry overnight, uncovered. Using a sharp knife dipped in hot water, cut into strips and then into diamonds. Remove from the board and coat with the caster sugar.

Store in a tin lined with baking paper, dusting with more sugar before sealing.

Makes approximately 100–150 pieces

Glossary

Ashkenazi Jews of Eastern European descent.

Babke A yeast cake.

blintzes Thin crepes with savoury or sweet fillings, which are then folded or rolled into parcels; of Eastern European origin.

bulka A sweet bun, often with cinnamon.

brocha(s) Literally a 'blessing', but in South African communities it is a get-together after synagogue.

bubba Grandmother.

chagim A collective term for Jewish festivals and holy days.

challah (pronounced HAH-lah) A traditional Jewish plaited bread prepared for festivals and Sabbath.

Chanukah The festival celebrating the 'miracle of the oil' from the first temple in Jerusalem. A great excuse to eat fried foods!

charoset A delicious combination of apple, walnuts, cinnamon and wine eaten at the Passover feast to represent the mortar used by the Jewish people when they were slaves in Egypt. Excellent on top of matzo.

chazzan A Jewish cantor who, among other things, leads the congregation in songs of prayer.

chrain The Yiddish word for horseradish condiment or relish, served as a garnish with gefilte fish. Can lift your lid like a good dose of wasabi.

cholent A traditional Jewish dish of (usually) meat, potatoes, beans and barley, which is made before Shabbath begins on a Friday, then slowly cooks all night and is served for lunch on Saturday.

fressing Eating with joy and abandon.

gefilte fish A traditional Jewish dish of minced and well-seasoned fish, which is made into patties and boiled in stock. Traditionally served with a slice of carrot on top and horseradish (chrain) on the side.

geschmirte matzo Matzo with a topping of cheesecake and cinnamon.

hamisher Simple, plain, tasty home cooking, or a down-to-earth person. Used as an adjective in a praising way.

kashrut The Jewish dietary laws. See also kosher.

kibbutz A communal way of living in Israel, originally for farming, but now for all sorts of businesses.

kichel A sweet cracker, typically eaten with a savoury topping like chopped herring.

kiddush (cup) Special blessing on wine (can also refer to the special cup, often silver or gold, used for this purpose).

kneidlach Also known as matzo balls; traditional Jewish dumplings made from matzo meal and eggs. Served in chicken soup at the Passover feast; can be cannonballs or floaters.

kosher If you keep kosher, you follow the Jewish dietary laws of kashrut; for example, not eating meat and milk products in the same meal, and not eating shellfish or pig products.

kreplach Pasta dumplings filled with meat to eat in chicken soup, like a Jewish ravioli.

matzo/matzo meal An unleavened bread, like a large square water cracker, eaten at Passover. Matzo meal is ground matzo and is available in coarse, fine or superfine varieties.

matzo brei A dish made at Passover of beaten eggs and soaked matzo, similar to scrambled eggs.

matzo kugel A pudding made from matzo, often sweet.

mohel The person who performs the Jewish rite of circumcision.

nachas The inexplicable joy one gets from something, often one's children.

omi/ouma Grandmother.

pareve A 'neutral' food that contains neither dairy nor meat ingredients. Kashrut forbids eating dairy and meat together in the same recipe or meal.

platta Hotplate, used to slow-cook meals overnight on Sabbath.

Pesach The eight-day festival of Passover where no bread is eaten to remember the days the Jews were slaves in Egypt. Our challenge is to cook and eat well without letting bread, flour or leavened products (chametz) pass our lips.

Rosh Hashanah The Jewish New Year, celebrated with many prayers and much feasting, particularly apples dipped in honey (for a sweet year) and too much honey cake.

sabra The term used for a Jewish person born in Israel.

savta A grandmother (Hebrew).

schmaltz The direct translation of this Yiddish word is 'fat'. In cooking, it is rendered chicken fat; on your body, it is the result of too much schmaltz in your cooking.

schmeared Our technical term for spreading, e.g. 'I schmeared chopped liver on a bagel'

Seder The customary feast held at Passover when Jewish people sit for hours, drinking wine, eating too much food and retelling the Passover story.

Sephardi Technically, Jews of Iberian Peninsula (now Spain and Portugal) descent, but nowadays includes Jews who are not Ashkenazi, for example of Iraqi, Indian and North African origin.

Shabbat The Sabbath, a day of complete rest. Begins at sunset on Friday and ends at sunset on Saturday; no work, much prayer and abundant eating.

Shavuot A festival celebrating receiving the Ten Commandments during which time we eat lots of cheesecake and cheese blintzes.

shidduch An arranged marriage or, colloquially, a successful introduction between two single people.

shul The Yiddish term for synagogue, the Jewish house of prayer.

simcha A celebration that pretty much always involves a huge amount of food.

sweet sacramental wine Also known as Kiddush wine, a sweet red wine used for blessing. In recipes, port can be substituted.

tsimmes/tzimmes A sweet Ashkenazi dish to celebrate New Year, usually with carrot and prunes and often with brisket.

WIZO (Women's International Zionist Organisation) A charity supporting women and children in Israel. www.wizo.org

Yiddish The old spoken language of many Ashkenazi Jews; a mix between German, Hebrew and other languages. Now it is mainly used by parents who don't want their children to understand what they are saying, and for those words that have no direct translation in English.

yiddishe mamma/nanna A woman who embodies the spirit of the old world in looking after her family and feeding them well.

Yom Kippur The Day of Atonement, when the Jewish people atone for their sins. It is a solemn day of fasting, which ends with yet another feast.

yomtov/yomtovim Festivals and holy days; literally means 'good day/s'. Yomtovim is the plural term.

Recipes by Courses

Biscuits and sweet treats

Passover

(v) = vegetarian
(gf) = gluten-free

Index

Acknowledgments

The MMCC project has been possible thanks to the immeasurable support from our wonderful husbands (who are still, miraculously, our husbands) and our (collective) seventeen children, who we all love very much. Thanks for understanding all our absences and distractions over the past years.

Great appreciation to the team at *Harper Collins Publishers* Australia, particularly Catherine Milne for her vision, faith and steadfast support; and editor Rachel Dennis for always getting the job done in her calm manner. Thanks to the committed team at HarperCollins 360, Victoria Comella and Jean Marie Kelly, for taking us to New York and beyond.

Huge thanks to our talented and generous creative team who managed to understand the contemporaneous ramblings of six passionate and obsessive women and still produce a beautiful book. To our brilliant photographer Alan Benson who continues to go above and beyond what's required and has become the brother in our sisterhood; to our very stylish food stylist David Morgan who brings a creative flair and knowing to everything he touches; to our lovely designer Tania Gomes who is so clever at getting it just right every time.

Thank you to Caroline (Lowry) Witts for helping us find the right pathway to this book; to Jane Lawson for her guidance and wisdom; to Rachel Quintana for helping us behind the scenes, day in and day out; to Nicole Wasserman and Louise Leibowitz for their editing and writing talents, easing our workload.

Thanks also to Markus Gerlich and OraKing Salmon, and the Biboudis clan from Birds Galore, Rose Bay North, whose contributions of fantastic produce always help support our charitable endeavours.

To Brenda, Barry and the whole crew at Bianca's, Rose Bay, who have sold our book and supported us since day one (and still continue to do so) by allowing us to donate all their book sale profits to charity; thanks also to Marshmellow boutique and Mandalay Flowers for supporting us through book sales; and to Hairbiz and Halo who not only sold our books but made our hair look fabulous as well!

Our continuing thanks to Tony Ryba of White International, a true friend of MMCC, who handles all our warehousing and transfers with no fuss at all. Thanks to our solicitors Arnold Bloch Leibler, our accountants and auditors MBP Advisory and our accountant Belinda Snape of Dakota Corporation for doing all the things needed to run a business that we have no idea how to do.

To Peter Ricci from Yakadanda, for creating our fabulous website and always being on the end of the phone to answer our never-ending questions.

To the following wonderful cooks who gave us extra-special help in the kitchen when we asked for it: Shereen Aaron, Danielle Barroukh (daughter of Colette Levy), Ruth Breckler, Ata Gokyildrim, Varda Goodman, Brenda Gordon, Judy Kaye, Debbie Levin, Charmaine and Deborah Solomon, Lena Toropova, Nikki Vernon, Esther Wakerman and Dinkie Wasserman.

Monday Morning Cooking Club is a not for profit company and 100 per cent of all our profits from sales of this book go to charity.

We thank WIZO NSW and WIZO Australia for their continued support.

Permissions

Breudher (page 208) and Chicken Everest (page 166) reproduced with permission from *The Complete Asian Cookbook* by Charmaine Solomon, published by Hardie Grant, 1976, completely revised and updated 2011

Balsamic lamb shanks (page 270) adapted and reproduced with permission from the recipe 'Balsamic rosemary and spanish onion braised lamb shanks' in the August 2002 issue of *Australian Gourmet Traveller*

Little honey cakes (page 282) adapted and reproduced with permission from the author Sophia Young

Chocolate orange cake (page 59) adapted and reproduced with permission from the recipe 'Chocolate orange cake' in *Feast* by Nigella Lawson, published by Chatto & Windus, 2004

Slow-cooked beef with ras el hanout (page 124) adapted and reproduced with permission from the recipe 'Slow-cooked beef with herbs' in *The Food of Morocco* by Tess Mallos, published by Murdoch Books, 2008

Middle Eastern kompot (page 137) reproduced with permission from Danielle and Dino Fossi from La Veduta, Russell, Bay of Islands, New Zealand

Visit us at www.mondaymorningcookingclub.com.au

HarperCollinsPublishers

First published in 2014
by HarperCollinsPublishers Australia Pty Limited
ABN 36 009 913 517
harpercollins.com.au

Text copyright © Monday Morning Cooking Club 2014
Photography copyright © Alan Benson 2014

The moral rights of the authors have been asserted.

HarperCollinsPublishers
Level 13, 201 Elizabeth Street, Sydney NSW 2000, Australia
Unit D1, 63 Apollo Drive, Rosedale, Auckland 0632, New Zealand
A 53, Sector 57, Noida, UP, India
77–85 Fulham Palace Road, London W6 8JB, United Kingdom
2 Bloor Street East, 20th floor, Toronto, Ontario M4W 1A8, Canada
10 East 53rd Street, New York NY 10022, USA

ISBN 978 0 7322 9781 7

Photography by Alan Benson
Design by Tania Gomes
Styling by David Morgan
Colour reproduction by Graphic Print Group, Adelaide
Printed and bound in China by RR Donnelley

5 4 3 2   14 15 16 17